RETURN TO PŌ

RETURN TO PŌ

JON-ERIK JARDINE

RETURN TO PŌ

ISBN   978-1-63676-574-7   *Paperback*

           978-1-63676-179-4   *Kindle Ebook*

           978-1-63676-183-1   *Ebook*

To my brother, may you journey far.

TABLE OF CONTENTS

———

Mai ka pō mai ka ʻoiāʻiʻo.
Truth comes from the night.
Truth is revealed by the gods.

ʻŌLELO NOʻEAU NO. 2067

AUTHOR'S NOTE

———

What brought me here? What drew me in and swept me away to this distant and mysterious place, a place teeming with life yet somehow existing in a realm beyond it? It is the place of night, the darkness where life emerged. A place where time itself was not yet created, and a time when space was only a murmuring chant across the blackness. It is a place where the oldest human stories are born, a time when the mysteries of life originated—where the gods call home.

In 2015, I packed up my entire life into ten sealed and quarantined five-gallon buckets, hopped on a ship, sailed across the entire fourteen-hundred-mile-long archipelago of Hawai'i, and landed on an uninhabited island—an atoll surrounded by a vast and isolating ocean. There I stayed for six months living and working in a landscape that was home to the world of seabirds. My job was to help restore the habitat for pacific marine life—life which was on the brink of extinction. Two years later in 2017, I returned—for what purpose I did not fully comprehend—and this experience ultimately prepared me for things in life that nothing else would.

The human experience of life takes on meaning only to the extent that life can be located within a storied universe, continually retelling itself. My life was nearing the end of a story—a death—and I was wandering around searching for a way, a meaning, to begin that story again.

Every journey into darkness is a return to a greater awareness of self. We are all burdened, yet simultaneously gifted, with an awareness of self. Life is full of paradoxes and puzzles that return us to our origin, reminding us to never forget how we exist in the first place, compelling us to search for something more than the living human world presents.

In the summer of 2018, my younger brother died in a drowning accident on a lake not far from our childhood home. With his death came a renewed sense of life and all we must do to keep life going, not just existentially but also symbolically, returning to the truth of who and what each of us are.

This is a series of personal essays about moving through the cycles of life, death, and renewal, beckoning forth a message for anyone who might sense something essential is missing from their own life. It is a story of environmental conservation and the hidden world of the wild pleading for wisdom. It is a story of adventure and the pursuit of the unknown. It is a story of teaching and mentorship. It is an exploration into how the cycle of a single human life may be fulfilled.

In writing this, I have depicted actual places, official agencies, cultural knowledge, and real people, all of which and whom exist in totality outside of the pages of this book. Within these pages, they are only representations, mere versions from my own limited perspective. These are my stories, my truths, and are not intended to be anything more than that. Yet I have tried my best to reach out to those this concerns the most because I believe all our truths are still connected, and thus, it is my responsibility to consider how my words may affect others.

I have decided to use Hawaiian names and terms as much as possible, to the extent of the knowledge I gained while living in Hawai'i. I feel it is important for the reader to build their own relationship to these words through my writing, a small way that I can help familiarize some of the Hawaiian language to a broader audience. I have provided a glossary of Hawaiian terminology. Included in the glossary are Hawaiian place names as well as the names of the many plants and animals I have encountered. There are a few words that are both the names of mythical figures and represent specific concepts depending on the context. The definitions or English translations are not meant to be comprehensive of that word but, rather, to give you a little understanding of how I am using them. I have italicized all of the Hawaiian words that are not the name of a place, person, or god.

As the mystery of life brought me to the island of Hawai'i, so too had the search for the unknown cast me beyond to the ancient and dying atoll of Hōlanikū, "bringing forth heaven."[1] I was a body of life, now preparing for its own departure into the realm of spirits.

---

1   Kekuewa Scott T. Kikiloi, "Kūkulu Manamana: Ritual Power and Religious Expansion in Hawai'i" (PhD diss., University of Hawai'i at Manoa, 2012), 49.

ANSWERING THE CALL

The tone in my stepfather's voice over the phone was enough for me to sense what would come next.

"Hi, Jon-Erik. It's Papa. I've got some bad news. Your brother went missing. We haven't heard from him since the Fourth."

My younger brother had run into trouble before as a high schooler. It wasn't a lot, more like a rough summer when school was out and the idleness of time inspired troublemaking, risk-taking behavior. He was the only one still living at home; the rest of us kids were all grown up. He had never gone missing before, not like this. Now he was in college and back home for the break, working his usual summer job at the lake renting boats out. But this time was different.

"The last we heard from him was at night," he continued. "He came home from a trip to the mall. Was in good spirits, talking about going down to the lake on his kayak to watch the fireworks. His kayak was found the next morning."

It would still take another forty-eight hours to know for sure what happened, but my body crumbled to the floor as soon as I hung up. My mind had lost nearly all of its agency. I was too dizzy to stand.

I stood up multiple times. Now my mind was whirling. It needed answers. It needed to know. What could have happened? Every possible outcome flashed through my head. Was he kidnapped? Was he lost somewhere? Already too many days had gone by since the Fourth.

There comes a time when innocence is shattered by loss and sorrow reigns over the land of the heart. I knew it would happen. It was bound to happen, as it always does and always will. All tied up in time, all our free will floating through life until it's time, I had been preparing for it. But I didn't know it. Somehow, all this living I was doing, all this searching and researching that spanned across oceans and pages of books, was to prepare for this moment. I just didn't know it would happen so soon. So abruptly. So unexpectedly.

I was living in Puna, Hawai'i that year, which sits on the most active volcano in the world, Kilauea, in a rustic development estate a few miles off the highway where dogs run loose and the streets were pitch black at night. I was twenty-eight. I had moved to this spot only a few weeks ago from the town of Hilo down east along the ocean. I was ready to get away from Hilo, the largest town on Hawai'i Island. With a population of only around eighty thousand people, it was still too large for me. I was used to much smaller places,

places where only a few people lived, so few you could count them on one hand.

I crawled to the door of the single-roomed cabin I was renting, opened it to the outside, and breathed for what felt like the first time in an eternity of drowning.

Drowning.

I was alone, save for the familiar *'apapane* honeycreeper birds singing in a nearby *'ōhi'a*, a uniquely adapted tree to the raw volcanic surface of Hawai'i. Bright, fiery red *lehua* blossoms scattered across its canopies to the delight of the *'apapane*. It was Friday, two days after the Fourth of July. The sun was out, but the ground was still soaked from the constant rain of the days before. The grass had grown long and wild, almost too tall for the mower I had hoped to use today.

I needed to not be alone. I needed someone to grab onto, to keep me afloat.

I wanted to call Taapai. He was my closest friend. I had met him during my first year living in Hawai'i, and we lived together on an old macnut orchard above Hilo that looked out on the town with the expansive ocean beyond. He was older than me, like most of my friends in Hawai'i, and was born and raised in Utah. He had spent some time in Tahiti, where his father was from, and he came to Hawai'i to try to get closer to a world he felt connected to. Our friendship grew over the years, sharing our passion for cultivating a closeness with the world in a way that seemed lost on many, drawn to the natural forces of life as if they spoke to us more clearly than the language of our own words. But Taapai was too far away at this point. My world was spinning, and the physical distance between us felt daunting. No longer living in Hilo, no longer living with Taapai, the twenty miles down into town felt like a journey away.

Billy and Alec lived just across the jungle road from me, two friends I met through the running community. They landed me the cabin I was living in, freeing me from the busy Hilo town. They were both teachers, something I was aspiring to become. Possibly one of them would be home in their own cabin since school was out for the summer. I fumbled around for my phone, finding it in my pocket.

"Are either of you home? I just found out my brother has been missing, and I think I need to be around somebody right now."

Billy was. He messaged back and told me to come by. I walked over, relieved. I tried to remain calm, conscientious the news of my brother could be upsetting, that the gritted and clenched agony striking across my face would be met with uncertainty and awkwardness. I walked over slowly, tightening the whole way over. I felt a hot prickle of selfishness creep up my body. Billy was probably having a nice relaxing evening, and now I was coming over rigid and on the verge of panic. Maybe that's all I wanted from Billy, just someone to act strong in front of as I battled the uncertain and yet inevitable outcome that was to come.

I told him what I knew, that my brother Taiga went out on the lake the evening of the Fourth to watch the fireworks. How his coworkers at the boat rental shop called the house when he did not show up for work the next day. That the police were called after a yoga instructor leading an early morning class at the lake found his kayak bobbing against the shore and brought it to the shop. How he had been texting our mother about how majestic the fireworks were, how grand it felt to be out on the lake surrounded by flashing lights in the sky reflecting below on the still dark water, like floating in the creation of the universe itself—a cascade of explosions illuminating the night.

I don't remember what happened next. I must have grown tired while walking back to my cabin under the now darkened skies. I don't remember the drive down into town the next day or meeting up with Taapai. It was as if I wasn't really here anymore. I felt suspended outside of time and space.

Taapai was waiting for me at the apartment he was staying in along the Keaukaha coast. I drove down the long Hawai'i belt road highway that gradually descended the forested slope of Kilauea volcano toward Hilo, a drive that left me feeling numb by the time I arrived. It was a sunny Saturday. I could hear families down at the rocky beach playing in the water and basking in the sun. I was relieved to see Taapai. He was the closest thing to home I had out here. He had met my whole family—even my brother, who once came out on his own to visit me when he was still in high school.

We spent the whole day together. He knew exactly what I needed: just someone to occupy this in-between world with this hollowed grief of unknown as I waited to hear my phone ring. I anchored myself to him, doing whatever he was doing that day.

We drove up the saddle to collect plants for the *hula halau* Taapai belongs to, the school where he studies and practices the ritual art of *hula* dancing. The highway was heavy with fog, leading up the saddle that sits between the meeting point of the two largest volcanoes in the world. Mauna Loa and Mauna Kea were hidden behind the veil of fog that moved through the canopy of trees, blanketing the forest with nurturing moisture. We came to walk among Laka, the goddess of the forest, to ask for her givings. Laka is the forest, present in the world as all which grows within the forest community.

She is the expression of that which grows. She is also the goddess of *hula*, and it is *hula* from which the forest is expressed. *Hula* is far beyond the scope of my comprehension, and although I had spent a few weeks joining the *halau* taapai dances as an introduction to a specific lineage of *hula* from the Pele clan, I was truly just a guest who would otherwise require years of cultivating a relationship with *hula* before I could really speak upon its behalf.

Taapai put me to work. I knew the plants we sought. We were collecting them to make *lei*, offerings and ordainments used in *hula* with the greatest intentions. Laka's shrine, called a *kuahu*, sits in every *hula halau* and is to always be dressed in fresh *lei* collected by the dancers who select specific plants that match a particular intention of that week. It was one of those connections we shared, drawn to the natural forces of life reflected in the unique intricacy of each plant that made up the native forest. He made sure to keep me active in my body so my mind would stay afloat. We were grounding ourselves in the practice of being fully present in a relationship with the place in which our bodies inhabited continuously. We weaved through thickets of *uluhe* ferns across jagged ancient lava flows now canopied by 'ōhi'a and *koa* tree forests. We collected *pukiawe* and *a'ali'i*.

We left the high forests and descended back into town, where the air was dense and warm. We stopped at the shores of *Keaukaha*, where Taapai encouraged me to get into the ocean. I soaked in the cool saltwater mixed with chilling fresh springs fed by underground aquifers formed over the ages. I glided through the transition from the hot muggy air into the refreshing pool. My mind let go of its clenching grasp. I swam under the surface, and everything felt as it should for just a moment, for just that one breath that lay trapped in my lungs as the sounds of the world above the surface were muffled.

I lifted myself out of the shallow water and sat on a lava rock, crossing my legs. I listened to the sounds of a nearby father playing with his daughter on the shore. A green sea turtle, *honu*, floated by, one I recognized as a resident of this particular beach park. The daughter reached out with some algae as an offering to the turtle. It approached the girl and inspected the algae, taking it graciously, but soon disposing of it. I looked under my crossed legs and found some sea purslane, *akulikuli*, growing in the cracks. I picked a stem and motioned for the young girl to try giving it to the *honu* instead.

"It's much more edible, see," I said as I took a bite myself. "I bet that *honu* will like it." She smiled and giggled, grabbing the *akulikuli* out of my outstretched hand. The *honu*, swimming in concentric circles, made its way back where the girl was squatting and reaching out with the newly acquired plant. The *honu* once again approached and politely took the *akulikuli* with its bill, this time disappearing behind its closed mouth.

Everything was as it should be.

I was surrounded by a congruent presence of life happily going about its own existence. The impending cascade of grief felt distant and out of focus. I was nothing more than simply alive among this father, his daughter, this *honu*, and this plant, somehow all intertwined in an exchange of offerings.

The *honu* moved on, and so did the family. I was left alone. I looked over to see Taapai had discovered some friends. A sinking feeling began to appear. The rock underneath me grew uncomfortable. Painful. I tried to ignore it, but it grew and grew until I felt like I was falling. I got up abruptly and signaled to Taapai I wanted to go.

I needed to go.

We made our way back to the apartment. I walked through the entrance and into the kitchen where my phone lay on the table. I picked it up. A message from my sister glared across the screen: *please call back.*

"Jon-Erik? Our brother is gone." Nothing more was said.

There is a lake near the house I grew up in. It is in the middle of the city. On all the hot summer days, my friends and I would walk down to the lake, cross the busy city traffic and through the park, and shed our sweaty street clothes and jump into its cold embrace. It is a small lake, and algae would bloom during those solstice days, making it fit for its name: Green Lake. That lake raised me and my sisters—and my brother.

But now it has taken one of our lives.

Two thousand and six hundred miles away, I awakened to a singular moment that changed my life forever. An exchange of life for death so far away, yet so certain, so absolutely real as if it happened right here in the apartment above the Hawaiian shores where a *honu* foraged for food and a young girl delighted in gifting its endeavors. Where the foraged gifts of the forest were being woven together into delightful *lei* as gifts for Laka. Where it was time, once again, to leave this place, this place of light near Kumukahi where the sun rises from the east to meet the day (*ao*) and venture into darkness (*pō*).

It was time to return to *pō*.

WHO I AM IS
WHERE I AM

———

I watched the sun rise above the Kilauea caldera. I watched it shine through the vapor that rises from geological steam vents, pouring out along the bluffs and dissipating over the rim of the caldera that sits above its sunken, desolate floor.

The reliable winds from the south and east whispered their gentle wavering gusts past my ears, catching the evaporated waters. A sped-up time-lapse of fog moved across the landscape as I sat in stillness alone in the early morning.

* * *

It was still dark out. My tent mate was sound asleep as I crawled out to greet the chilly tropical morning air. We were camping at four thousand feet. There was a slight scent of sulfur, mixed with the aroma of eucalyptus trees that buffeted our campsite from the trade winds and the nearby highway. Throwing on layers, I glanced around and noticed the still quietness of our group, stretched out across the grass in various-sized silhouetted tents under a waxing moon. No one was awake, save me. I wanted to keep it that way.

I snuck my running shoes on, fumbling to tie the damp and dewy laces in the dark, and eagerly set off to find the mouth of one of the most active volcanoes on Earth.

Within the caldera is the Halema'uma'u crater, home of the passionate goddess of fire, Pele: she-who-shapes-the-sacred-land. I sat perched at the site where Pele's brother, Kamohoali'i, god of the shark, is meant to live. Pele gave him this cliff, Palikapuokamohoali'i, for helping her navigate to the island of Hawai'i from Kahiki. It is said she gifted him with this side of the caldera where no smoke or fumes ever blow.[2]

I used the light of the moon to find my way up the trail across hardened lava rock. We were only camped a half a mile away, and the glow from the molten lake lit up the horizon, casting the sparse shrubs and trees into stark shadows. I was fully awake now, natural adrenaline kicking in from my limited sight of the surrounding darkness and the sense of the unknown as I moved closer and closer toward the

---

2   Harry Nimmo, *Pele, Volcano Goddess of Hawai'i: A History* (Jefferson: McFarland & Company, Inc., Publishers, 2011), 24.

light, my heavy breathing shattering the silence that filled this cavity.

I was happy to get away from the group. It had only been a day since we all arrived, meeting for the first time at the Hilo International Airport. I was shy and anxious, already filled with doubt and dread about my decision to join this eight-week environmental science college program. We were here for the interest of studying the wildlands of Hawai'i through the hands-on lens of science. I didn't know if I was as interested in the academic opportunity of this program as much as I was looking for an excuse to get away from the growing confusion of my life back home.

The path opened up, and I found myself in an empty parking lot with the Halema'uma'u crater glowing red on the far side. I made my way over, catching my breath. A thin line of light was painting the horizon a light blue, spreading up toward the stars and the moon. I couldn't see the edge yet, but I could sense it was close with the crater glowing brighter and brighter.

Suddenly, there it was, off in the distance, now a few hundred feet below me. I had climbed up and up the trail from camp to stand above and stare down into a crater of creation that came from the center of the Earth.

I gazed out and pictured myself as the shark god. I looked down below in the crater where my sister Pele lives. I imagined the rain pouring down the slopes of Mauna Loa, seeping into the ground, down toward the lava, toward Pele where her fiery passion vaporizes, steaming through the cracked vents, bellowing out over my head and over the rim of the giant caldera, and fading with the rising sun. I saw myself in the middle of all of this, witnessed it all happening around me. I couldn't help but feel as if I was part of this story. I imagined myself as part of the land and wondered how I could feel so at home when I was thousands of miles away from all those I had ever known and ever loved.

In that moment, in that stillness where only a few hundred feet below rumbled and stirred the raw insatiable chaos of creation, I realized I did not want to return to where I came from. Back there, I had no story to hold on to, no thread of the past weaving into my present, connecting me from what is to what once was. I wanted to be a part of this place, here on the newest formation of land in the world, so active and alive with myth.

But how does one make a new place home?

I returned down the slope from the rim of the caldera to our campsite. Everyone was just getting up, slowly emerging from their tents, standing and stretching and taking in the new day. Pele's wavering temper lingered in my mind. I thought about what the volcanologists we visited the other day told us about the volcanic activity. They shared how volcanism is a widely theoretical discipline. The anomaly of hotspots such as the one generating magma in the mantle layer of the earth directly below Hawai'i Island is not understood very well. No one knows for certain why the subterranean magma inflates and deflates when it does, eventually erupting out of the surface of the volcano through vents.

Many years later in the spring of 2018, only months before my brother's death, while teaching part-time at a middle school along the Hamakua Coast of Hawai'i Island, the ground of the classroom began to shake and continued shaking for half a minute. We all knew it was the volcano; magma that had been swelling inside the crater called Pu'u O'o on the slopes of Kilauea had drained rapidly. It was observed heading through subterranean passageways down toward the Puna shores. The earthquake we felt must have been some kind of eruption. All that lava had broken through the surface, fissuring out of the ground. It was exhilarating but also meant that destruction would follow.

Time itself transported me back to the mythic beginnings of these islands when Pele first arrived in Hawai'i nei, establishing her new home right here in this volcano. She would take trips down from her home in the Halema'uma'u crater to the shores of Puna, down to her favorite spot of Ha'ena, entertained by the swaying *hala* trees that danced as the wind from the ocean blew through their leaves.[3]

Pele came from Kahiki, a place commonly thought of today as Tahiti. She left her home under the direction of her mother, Haumea, to find her father, Kānehoalani, here in Hawai'i. In her search, she was confronted by her older sister, Nāmakaoakaha'i, who, back in the world of Kahiki, had sought to destroy Pele for her unrelenting power and ambition. Pele's journey on the mythic canoe Honuaiākea was a journey of refuge to escape the threats of her older sister. The passage of her journey, which was taken with the company of other relations of Pele, brought the voyage first to the northwest islands of Hawai'i. Pele made her way down the islands, using the divine rod Paoa to determine where she would land and call her new home. Pele surveyed each island, each location resulting in dissatisfaction. Upon her examination of the crater of Haleakala volcano on Maui, Pele's older sister, Nāmakaoakaha'i, confronted her after trailing her throughout the whole journey. The two sisters went into

---

3   Nathaniel Bright Emerson, *Pele and Hiiaka: A Myth from Hawaii* (Hilo: Edith Kanaka'ole Foundation, 2015), 1-2.

battle, Nāmakaoakaha'i determined to destroy Pele. Alas, Pele was bested by her sister and violently dismembered.[4]

In this act, the ancient person that was Pele came to an end, but her being in that moment became deified as a goddess, now functioning as the creator of land. She left Maui and made her way to Hawai'i Island, eventually settling at Halema'uma'u crater.[5]

There are only theories about the swelling and increased pressure in the magma chamber, theories that circulate in discussions among scientists but never reach any conclusion.

As the sulfur smell flooded my nostrils, I smiled with a wild yet comforting thought that it was, of course, Pele who was causing all of the eruptions.

---

4   Emerson, *Pele and Hiiaka*, XIV-XV.

5   Ibid.

WAVES OF WAIMANU

In 2013, I had moved to the Big Island of Hawai'i, Hawai'i Island, Moku O Keawe. In 2018, my brother died. Within the five-year period between my initiation into Hawai'i and my brother's death was a notable separation period from my own past, the time of "betwixt and between."[6] I was neither here nor there.

We had a late start, running on island time. We'll get there when we get there. Time in the tropics was less apparent, less relevant. We came to the valley to escape it. Down

---

6   Victor W. Turner, *The Forest of Symbols* (New York: Cornell University Press, 1967), 93-111.

into the valley we would go, and down below where time could not reach us.

But we wouldn't escape the ticking approach of limitations. Every valley has a bottom. What goes up must come down.

It looked to be a busy day in the valley, a clear and sunny day. But it wouldn't stay that way. We stuffed our backpacks with provisions, not taking the time to be careful, only to be carefree.

We threw on our packs. We made sure the car was locked and parked at the top, a place called Koa'e kea, named after the white-tailed tropic bird, and began the descent into the first valley called Waipi'o.

I had just gotten off another eight straight days of work. I was in my usual zombie state. The contrast between going so many days in a row leading a group of young adults through an intentionally emotional and physically taxing journey and my own slow island lifestyle always left me feeling quite unsure of how to wake up and reorient. I was relieved not to have to be constantly vigilant of the whereabouts and conditions of the young adults pushing the limits of who they are.

It would prove to be one of my last shifts. Daniel, my accompanied friend for the hike, had already quit, and it seemed I was destined for the same. We were finished, spent, but I didn't know that yet. I could only sense something building inside. It had been a tough week. Daniel knew it, and he could see it on me—the distant look in my face, the gravity on my shoulders. So we decided to hike into Waimanu to get away from it all, to be rejuvenated by the majestic valleys of Kohala.

The road got steeper. Our bodies adjusted to the grade while bearing the load of our packs. Large four-wheel-drive trucks rolled up and down the road revving in their high gears and blasting that slow, rhythmic island music. We stayed on the edge, where only a thin metal barrier separated us from plunging hundreds of feet down to the valley floor.

This was Waipiʻo Valley, situated on the north side of Kohala, the oldest of the five volcanoes that make up Hawaiʻi Island. Being the oldest, it has eroded over time into a series of deeply cut valleys, Waipiʻo being the largest.

We made it to the bottom, our quads burning from the hike. The rolling shore break greeted us with the back and forth sounds of rocks being pulled down from the beach and the crashing of waves on top.

We approached the mouth of the river—rain collected from Kohala all the way down into the valley, the mixing of freshwater and saltwater—the meeting place of two worlds born into the next, combining their nutrients. Daniel stopped to take his pack off. I followed suit, happy to remove the weight. We stood in front of the ocean that spanned out beyond the edges of the valley and into the horizon. Our hot prickly skin cooled as our hearts slowed their beating and the trade winds wicked the sweat off our bodies.

The burdened week of work started to dissipate but then tightened its hold on me again. Those young adults' lives, some just a few years younger than I, some a little older, were in my hands—their vision of a hopeful future mediated by my guidance.

The waves crashed onto the shore, grinding against the lava rock.

The students made masks for each other, lying down under the sun for a full hour, breathing quietly and relaxing every muscle to avoid distorting the shape of the mask while their partner added one strip after the next onto their face, sculpting a rough but accurate representation of all the contours that make up the structure of their profile. We let the masks dry overnight, talking over a fire about how they wanted to paint them and what symbols they wanted to illustrate. Their masks were meant to represent all their fears and traumas, everything that was holding them back, and the weight of responsibility pressed in on me.

The waves pulled back toward the ocean, dragging the rocks down the shore, and tossing them with immense ease.

Watching the waves, I choked down the knots rising from my gut, swallowing the fear and chaos that threatened to erupt. It was just a shore break, nothing more. I was just a facilitator of a rites-of-passage program, not a reckoning force of ocean and land engaged in a forceful transformation for these coming-of-age adults.

The program was inspired by the emergence of wilderness therapy as an alternative solution for rehabilitating adolescents and young adults inflicted with a wide range of mental health and behavioral issues: anxiety, depression, anger and defiance, isolation, computer and gaming addiction, drug addiction, family conflicts, learning differences and social differences, lack of self-esteem or confidence, grief and loss, entitlement, academic underachievement, negative peer groups, and so on. They had so many diversions from the path forward, and so many paths that could lead to perpetual harm, or even death.

Adolescence through the ages has always been understood as a turbulent time. It is the transition between the major existential identities. A child comes to know of themself as a child in relationship to their family and community, all the while knowing someday they will grow up to be an adult. But the child does not understand fully how this will occur, nor if they will be ready for it. As the body of a child continues to grow and mature, the child still lives through this identity, constantly wondering how and when they will feel or see themselves as an adult. It is a transformation that does not happen on its own, yet the transformation is beckoned forth, called upon, by some inner-working force. What happens if we do not answer the call?

The smell of burning sage snapped me back.

My nose turned toward the scent and my gaze followed to see Daniel standing at the edge of the river as it flowed into the ocean and the ocean swept into the river. I knew what this was, and I found myself immediately wanting to reject his intentions.

He was beginning to enact a rites-of-passage ritual for our overnight trip into Waimanu, the next valley over. It was a ritual we had learned through our work adopted from the School of Lost Borders Vision Fast, a pan-cultural rite of passage in the wilderness. In actuality, rites of passage as a process has been around much longer than the existence of any present culture, having been passed down through generations, adapting and evolving to fit the contemporary relevance of any one culture and its relationship to the natural world.

The term "rites of passage" itself did not exist until the early 1900s, coined by the ethnographer Arnold van Gennep who developed it into a three-stage model of separation, transition, and incorporation (roughly speaking) to wholly represent the universality of transformation.[7] This now-abstracted

7   Arnold van Gennep, *The Rites of Passage Second Edition,* trans. Monika B. Vizedom and Gabriel L. Caffee (Chicago: University of Chicago Press, 2019), 21.

concept was later popularized by Joseph Campbell in his 1949 book *The Hero with a Thousand Faces*, a comprehensive look at how this cultural phenomenon has emerged across cultures through the human commonality of storytelling and ritualization of those stories into a lived experience for the initiate.[8]

Now Daniel was doing the same, creating a metaphysical space in which we would enter as soon as we crossed the threshold, which Daniel demarcated as the river—very appropriate as rivers constitute natural boundaries and, thus, are symbolic of a crossing into other psychological realms.

I now knew this trip wasn't going to be easy. It was going to be a confrontation. I had a lot to confront that I had been pushing away for some time now.

* * *

I came to Hawaiʻi to live and to work. I became a guidance counselor at a wilderness therapy organization where I reunited with Daniel, whom I had befriended when we were in college. We took similar classes that lured us with their descriptions of the boundlessness of the body's primary experience of the world and the way culture shapes the mind to interpret these experiences.

I joined Daniel in leading a workshop for incoming students on a basic exercise for removing stress from the body. We based it on Robert Sapolsky's work on how stress and anxiety function in the body. He describes how they are natural responses to our environment, yet our modern functionality

---

8   Joseph Campbell, *The Hero with a Thousand Faces* (Navato, California: New World Library, 2008), 6-18.

prevents our minds from turning down the stress response, causing a chronic system of stress to pour through our bodies.[9] Daniel and I connected in sharing the same desire to integrate the latest findings in modern Western science with practices that had been traditionally ritualized in cultures that predate science. We were fascinated with learning the healing dance of the Kalahari Ju|'hoansi, who enact rituals mimicking the shaking behavior of prey animals who lay down and twitch after surviving being hunted and chased by a predator, allowing built-up static energy to be released.[10]

Through this connection, Daniel and I ended up on a similar path. Daniel came to Hawai'i just two months after I arrived to begin working at the same therapy company. I met him at the downtown bus stop in Hilo and walked him to the shores of the island after he expressed a need to immerse himself as soon as possible in the waters of this place. "To introduce myself," he explained. But he didn't need to explain it. We already shared this understanding, and we worked our way through to become the lead facilitators for the rites-of-passage stage of the program in Hawai'i.

The concept of rites of passage wasn't new to me, but my understanding of it was vague. I had learned of it as most people do—a cultural observation of the natural cycles of life playing themselves out in our personal lives. The seasons encapsulate the entirety of this cycle. When I spent a summer in the Appalachian Mountains of North Carolina as a

---

9   Robert Sopolsky, *Why Zebras Don't Get Ulcers* (New York: Henry Holt and Company, LLC, 1994), 41-56.

10 Richard Katz, Megan Biesele, and Verna St. Denis, *Healing Makes Our Hearts Happy, Spirituality and Cultural Transformation among the Kalahari Ju|'hoansi* (Rochester: Inner Traditions International, 1997), 18-20.

counselor for an experiential learning and wilderness camp, I learned of the Medicine Wheel, a healing and knowledge system accredited to many peoples around the world and perhaps most notably the Plains Tribes in America, although it is not limited to any one nation or tribe. But it begins with a circular way of examining the world.

John Fire Lame Deer of the Lakota Tribe writes of cyclical thinking, referring to it as "the hoop":

"To our way of thinking the Indian's symbol is the circle, the hoop. Nature wants things to be round. The bodies of human beings and animals have no corners. With us, the circle stands for the togetherness of people who sit with one another around the campfire, relatives, and friends united in peace while the pipe passes from hand to hand. The camp in which every tipi had its place was also a ring. The tipi was a ring in which people sat in a circle, part of the larger hoop, which was the seven campfires of the Sioux, representing one nation. The nation was only part of the universe, in itself circular and made of the earth, which is round; of the sun, which is round; and of the stars, which are round. The moon, the horizon, the rainbow—circles within circles with no beginning and no end. To us, this is a beautiful and fitting symbol and reality at the same time, expressing the harmony of life and nature. Our circle is timeless, flowing; it is new life emerging from death - life winning out over death."[11]

This Medicine Wheel is both a ceremonial practice and an understanding of how we move through natural stages continuously from birth to death by orienting this movement

---

11   John Fire and Richard Erdoes, *Lame Deer: Seeker of Visions* (New York: Simon Schuster, 1994), 110-111.

into a concentric cycle, like a wheel or hoop, in the same direction as the sun, or rather our Earth's spin, to sync up the movement through life stages with the cosmic and natural cycles of our world.

The trade winds blowing in from the north entered through the cliffs of the valley walls and hit the burning sage in Daniel's hand, sending the smoke spiraling up toward the sky. Daniel stood along the edge of the river, which now cut a fast-moving pass into the beach and out to the crashing waves, separating us from our journey toward Waimanu, beckoning us to step into its fast but shallow currents.

He let the sage burn for a long time. I joined him at the edge of the river, letting the smoke fill my nostrils, letting the river water gurgle below me, letting the nearby waves thunder beside me, and letting the wind spin and twist around me. The world and I felt mixed and spiraled together—the salt, the smoke, the sounds, the ocean spray. My life as a continuum collided and extended in reverberation, and I stood upon the threshold held in the suspense of my own silence, drowned away by the emergence of all that was surrounding me. The stage was set, and now our bodies were fully cued into a transition from one phase to the next.

Based on these observed stages, Kenneth Wilber, founder of the Institute for the Integral Stage of Human Development, contributed to developing what is called "spiral dynamics"—a theory that shows humans evolving or developing through eight major waves of consciousness. These eight stages form a spiraling structure that encapsulates not only the developing stages of an individual but also of populations as humanity itself is evolving through eras of societal changes.[12] Cultures which have observed these cycles in nature have observed them in humans, actively building cultural tools of initiation to help us identify when it is time for a member of that group to pass through into the next stage and how to appropriately acknowledge that transition as a means for psychological and spiritual activation. Thus, we spiral forward from birth until death, like an entire galaxy as it floats through the surrounding blackness of space.

These rites-of-passage ceremonies vary greatly, but often have an element of removing the initiate from their home (home representing the safety and stability of society) and are thrusting them into the bush, the forest, or the desert, which represents the unknown, the cosmos, and death, to accomplish tasks on their own. Many of these initiations have an element of a test the initiates must pass to be accepted back into the community, and when they do, they are celebrated and acknowledged as full members of the community. They are no longer just a dependent child. For example, the Inuit peoples of Alaska would take their children on their first hunting trip with the expectation it was time for the child to hunt for food. It is this process that enables the psyche of an individual to metaphysically transform into a new and established identity as an adult: independent and capable of taking on a role of responsibility and accountability in the community.

These confrontations with the wilderness assert a degree of danger. Failure to accomplish the task can often be met with death; at the very least, initiates must feel as if death is

---

12   Kenneth Wilber, A *Theory of Everything* (Berkley: Shambhala Publications, 2000), 5-13.

an imminent possibility if they do not succeed. The possible design of these ceremonies is to activate the psychological state of confrontation with death as a means of understanding what is entailed in true transformation as well as imparting the seriousness and gravity of what it means to be a physically, psychologically, and spiritually mature being. The isolation is key in recognizing the lesson can't be learned from anyone; it can only be learned through one's own journey into a confrontation with death.

The rites of passage at the therapy program followed this basic design. My task as a lead facilitator was to execute the design as best as I could, to make it meaningful and demonstrate who they are now and who they are becoming are two different worlds, and that they must cross from one to the next consciously and courageously.

I took a deep breath and told myself to trust the process. The fringe of my struggles came into focus as I exhaled and accepted Daniel's initiation of our own rites of passage. The exhausting eight-day, thirteen-hour shifts compiled of monitoring and facilitating, the anticipated trauma and heavy energy as I guided these young adults into their own rites of passage, and the burden weighing on my conscience of what I was exposing these young adults to suddenly all flashed in front of me, and that wave of uncertainty swept through me once again.

I stood now at the gates of the river threshold and silently stated my intentions, desiring clarity. I was desiring to face the source of my troubling hesitance to pursue a role I previously felt had been my calling. A question appeared in the silence: did I not feel worthy of this role?

Daniel put out the sage and we crossed the river, taking off our boots and slinging them around our necks. We had entered the world between worlds. It was time to hike out of Waipiʻo, traverse across the nine miles of gulches and ravines to the isolated deep valley of Waimanu.

We zigzagged up the far valley wall of Waipiʻo and trudged ahead, eager to get to the top. At every turn on the switchbacks, our view opened up and we could see more and more of the valley. Giant waterfalls, *wailele*, hid behind ridge-lines, nourishing the valley. Up and up we went, silently, save for the heavy breathing between each carefully placed step.

The main part of the students' rites-of-passage experience was the three-day solo. They would spend the entirety of it by themselves, and they had to build their own shelters to protect from the elements and eat a limited diet. There could be no distractions from confronting the change they wished to instill in their lives moving forward. In today's world, spending three days alone is extremely uncommon, and most of us would find it very challenging. Adding to this experience are the ritual layers of transformation and the intentional initiatory rites of shelter-building and fasting were designed to create an experience that would both heighten and deepen each student's awareness of their own authentic self.

We emerged at the top, nearly one thousand feet up from the ocean surface where the crashing waves now looked small and gentle, but still sounded like distant thunder. The shade of the non-native pine trees was a welcomed retreat from the oppressive sun, but the mosquitos that also enjoyed the cooler air were not, and so we soon found ourselves on our way again, snaking along the trail.

In the silence, our intentions germinated and grew into tendrils of conscious-aware thoughts. I began cycling through the students who went through the rites-of-passage program. It was the first group of students I had led since they first came into the program weeks before. I was attached to their outcomes. We had built up memories together, and I had learned a lot about their lives as we developed a trusting rapport.

The moments of those days played through my mind: driving out to the camp, banging a slow steady beat on a hand drum they followed blindfolded up to the ipu-trellised threshold, going through each ritual to prepare them for the seventy-two-hour solo. The entire camp was nestled on a parcel of land on the south side of the island. What once used to be a dirt bike track was now shaped into a tropical garden surrounded by tall cane grass and beyond that a thick, messy forest of vines and introduced trees. At the center of the camp were the remnants of an old giant bike jump that had been dug out into a pit, like a crater, like a circle.

I beat the drum to call them back from their solo site where they had been working to construct shelters made of bamboo and a tarp. They joined me where I was perched at higher grounds, where I would sit and watch over each of their sites during their solo.

They trickled out slowly, obviously fatigued from the lack of sustenance. We gathered around the circular crater that represented the cycles of life. I pointed to the west, indicating the place of death, where the sun sets and where all life goes to die—the realm of pō. I spoke, breaking what had been a sacred silence, and said, "Before you entered your solo, I asked each of you to write your own eulogy as if you truly had died. I asked you to imagine what your loved ones would have to say about you. I did not tell you what we would be doing with this. Now, the time has come to show you."

They traced every word uttered from my lips, looking for any clues of what was going to happen next. Their gaze was both one of deep tiredness but also fear. My heart was beating hard.

"Remain where you are until you hear the beating of the drum," I said dispassionately. I disappeared behind a wall of grass, finding the trail that led to a small enclosure. In the center lay an open grave, a rough dugout section in the earth a few feet deep, just wide and long enough to fit one person laying down.

An altar was set up at its head, full of skulls and bones and other symbols of death. I draped myself in black robes and painted my face blood red and dark black. The heat of the sun and the sweat from my pores melted and mixed the paints into a mosaic of crude chaos, the dripping of sweat beads streaming lines down my chin as if my face was caught in an eternal cry of sorrow.

I could see their frightened gaze when they emerged through the overgrown cane grass, some with eyes opened wide in dismal surprise, others frowned and looked away. I could hear the tremble in their voices, standing around the grave, when they read aloud the letters to their loved ones. Their voices were quiet, distant, as if the words they recited were already severed from their own existence, fading into the drowning hum of insects.

They took turns lying inside the grave and wearing their masks, the embodiment of death, the veil that hides their true potential, the dead wood that must be burned, enclosing them like a tomb, as I read aloud their eulogies, as they lay in the Earth, speaking out their own solemn words that rang out and cascaded down onto them, pressing them further and further into the earth.

I relived that week in my head. It made me dizzy. I started breathing harder. Daniel, who was leading the way, stopped at a creek.

"Hey, let's take a break, maybe grab some water," he suggested. I nodded in agreement, trying to hide my state of mind, but Daniel looked at me inquisitively.

"I'll pump the water, you just rest," he said.

I found a smooth and cool boulder in the small creek. The sound of the water coming down from an endless stream connected with my thoughts, pouring them out until the world around me ceased to exist.

The strongest memories I have of my brother are from childhood. We shared a room. We shared our toys. We shared our adventures. I shared what I knew, and he followed along, always catching on quickly, determined to become just as good at whatever we were building or playing.

During his memorial, my friends walked up to me to share their own childhood memories of him. My brother would always tag along, joining in whenever he could—throwing beanie babies at each other in the basement behind barricades of pillows. They'd share how, at the age of three or so, my brother would show up to the dinner table without a shred of clothes on and proudly exclaim, "Get naked!" before taking his time circling the table and stopping to reach up and fondle each person's earlobe while he sucked his thumb.

Those memories would make me smile and laugh. But they were all from his early years. I had no memories to share from his recent life. It's as if he had just stopped being a part of my life.

Or I stopped being a part of his.

I seemed to know my brother less and less as he got older. Eventually, I felt like I barely knew him.

* * *

My foot slipped off the wet rock and into the cool creek water, soaking my shoe. I took my backpack off, facing away from Daniel. He took notice and approached.

"What's going on?"

I broke down. Halfway to our destination, halfway along the journey, right when things were the hardest.

I cried, my whole body shuddering. One large river carving out a whole valley and crashing into a whole ocean, mixing, stirring, and swirling.

Daniel let me cry. Then he pushed me. "Tell me. What is frustrating you? Get it out. Say it. Claim it!"

So I did. I told him how wrong it all felt. How I was affecting all these young adults' lives, but who was I to judge if it was for the best? I had never put myself through such a challenge, I hadn't yet answered the call. I, too, was a young man trying to confront a world much larger than myself and was still in the midst of my own limited breadth of experience. It wasn't right. It had to stop. Maybe it was thoughts of my brother's recent visit that same year and the distance I felt from his life. The impact I was having on these young adults who were unknown to me up until this year and how I thought I knew my brother up until his visit—I didn't seem to have control over any of it.

It was starting to get late. The light was beginning to change quickly, even as we continued hiking in the shady understory of the guava trees lining the sides of the trail.

A few miles later, we emerged out of the brush to see the lonely valley of Waimanu stretched below us with the sun beginning to fall behind the other side. We strapped on our headlamps and began the last descent, passing through the twisting *hala* trees with their long wide fronds and serrated edges, down through the *palapalai* ferns still moistened by the humid air, down across another river with a rope tied across to help from falling, keeping me upright as I crossed over the turbulence that threatened to wash me out into the ocean.

It was dark when we arrived, and the winds had picked up. We could barely hear each other before the rain began. Daniel's headlamp stopped working. We worked together under my single light, setting up our hammocks and tarps, one by one. Famished and dehydrated, we scraped together a modest dinner before scattering to our respective hammocks. The storm was at full force now, deafening winds and falling rain amplified by the trees as their myriad of branches and leaves rattled together. I clambered inside my hammock and wrapped myself up.

ALL THE WAY UP THE CHAIN TO HŌLANIKŪ

The bazaar was busy with people moving in every which direction. A bright day shined on the commerce of humanity. Every item imaginable was displayed under canvas tents stretching out along endless rows. The limitless transactional possibilities were infinite entrails of human valuables.

Among the currents of merchants and buyers, I spotted two figures of similar height standing side-by-side facing me, but their faces were blurred by the constant movement of people passing by.

I was intrigued by them, how they stood in purposeful stillness as everyone else seemed caught in perpetual motion. I was drawn to them and approached. As I did, the busyness of the bazaar appeared to dwindle and clear out while the two figures remained.

I could see their faces now: my two fathers.

I cocked my head, humored, if not perplexed.

This was odd.

What were they doing here? Why were they together? Smiling, they turned and looked at each other, then back at me, gesturing me over.

The bazaar, now deserted, was filled with an overwhelmingly peculiar feeling I couldn't shake. My two fathers joined hands and turned to exit the market. I followed willingly and unwillingly, seemingly guided by an agency that existed beyond my own sense of self.

We entered a house that sat on the corner of a cobbled road. It was unlit and unfurnished, just an empty space defined only by the dimensional boundaries of an enclosure. My fathers walked to the back of the empty space where stairs lead us down underground.

We were moving through a dark and moist passageway. The air was cold yet comforting. Water dripped from above. I could just make out the shadowy figures of my fathers as they guided me through the tunnel. I felt the soft and squishy ground beneath my feet and reached my arms out to touch the wet sides of the tunnel that met the tips of my fingers.

Our tunnel soon opened up into another room. It appeared to be dark like a cellar but had light streaming through cracks in floorboards above. At the opposite end of the cellar was another set of stairs and standing in front of the stairs were another set of figures. I couldn't quite make them out in the darkness. My fathers beckoned me forth in the direction of the two figures guarding the stairs.

It seemed this was as far as my fathers would go. I waved goodbye without saying anything and walked up to the new figures, who I now saw were dressed in all-white gowns.

They were two elderly women with long white hair to match their clothes. I did not recognize them, but they seemed to know me, or at least expected me, for they stepped aside and allowed enough space for me to walk past.

I opened the door at the top of the stairs. Light flooded out from the other side, blinding me as I entered. A brightly lit and wonderfully warm room appeared before me. As my eyes adjusted, the shape, form, and function of the room fell into place. It was some kind of workroom, like a woodshop. An arrangement of tables filled the room with toys, trinkets, and the sorts, half-built, lying scattered across each surface. Light seemed to be emanating from everywhere and nowhere. In the middle of all of it stood a small and thin, rosy-cheeked man whose large smile left no room for his eyes.

A joyful silence bounced between the rosy-cheeked man and me. I gazed at him with delight as the workshop of creations around us pulsed to the beat of my heart. After a timeless period, and before it, the rosy-cheeked man opened his smile and uttered the clearest words I had ever heard:

"Now, you must meditate on Brahma."

* * *

The wind had calmed down since the hours before when I drifted asleep in my swaying hammock underneath a bustling tarp. I could just hear the grinding and rolling of large, smooth stones being pushed and pulled by the constant turbulence of waves mingling with the shore. A rhythmic beat penetrated my eardrums and reverberated in the cavities of my body. The stars were brilliant speckles piercing through the ironwood and *kamani* canopy cover. The dark loom of the steep valley walls enveloped my peripherals. A single word dripped from my lips in a steady repeat.

Brahma. Brahma. Brahma.

I caught myself uttering the word like a strange chant, coming into full consciousness, shaken awake by the verbal resonance. A vivid memory of my dream came flowing through the ether, passing through my vision like light projecting through rolling film.

The storm had cleared and the swaying *hala* trees lifted and twirled with the wind as it steadily pushed onto shore. I unraveled from my cocooned hammock, reborn into the day. The ground was still wet from last night's rain, but the sky had opened up, revealing its blue hue.

I walked out to the shore where the humming waves met the rocky beach, taking a seat on a pile of porous rocks, smoothed and worn over. I traced the word *Brahma* with my mouth over and over.

I wasn't sure I had heard the word before. Perhaps I had while overhearing someone talking. Now it is a word I am more familiar with than most; it's unforgettable. But then I practiced saying it, unsure if I was even pronouncing correctly, unsure if it was an actual word. Its meaning was as mysterious as creation itself.

My brother was a sophomore in high school during my time acting as a rites-of-passage facilitator. The summer before, I was working in the Appalachians at a summer wilderness camp. It was an outdoor education center where children could come to be immersed in the woods and learn wilderness skills like how to make fires, forage for edible foods in the forest, carve wood and build shelters, and navigate with just a compass. It was also an education center that hosted kids who grew up in the foster care system. I was mentoring adolescents on how to be in the woods and, thus, how to be in the world. I was just entering adulthood, and all I wanted to do was help those who were most at risk of not making it into stable adulthood. While I looked for opportunities to do this, I never considered maybe I could have helped my own brother as well. He was sometimes getting into trouble back home.

But I was all the way across the country. It pained me. I understood why he was making the decisions he was at such a young age. I also got into trouble when I was a teenager— running from cops at parties in public parks, sneaking out and getting high with friends in vacant dark lots. Maybe my brother was just unlucky.

The smell of nutty oats drifted from behind me and my stomach awoke, distracting me from that single word and the thoughts that followed. It would be the first of an endless thread of meditations on Brahma. I lifted myself from the black volcanic rocks and made my way back to camp where Daniel was finishing up cooking our breakfast.

I perched myself on top of a log surrounding the camp stove as Daniel served me oats. I took the bowl, staring out into the space between my portion and the pot of porridge, the source of our cooked sustenance.

As Daniel began to serve himself, I asked him, "Does the word 'Brahma' mean anything to you?"

Daniel finished scooping the steaming cereal into his bowl, a slight pause before his response, as if he was bringing forth something deep from within. "It does," he said. I waited for him to say more, my heart leaping with only the most subtle change not even I noticed.

When he was sixteen, my parents flew my brother Taiga out to visit me. I don't think I realized how young my brother really was when he visited. Only sixteen years old, Taiga excelled at school when he cared, but that was rare. His teachers knew he was smart, or at least the ones who cared knew. He was the kind of student who rarely turned in completed assignments but nearly always aced his tests. It just didn't seem like high school was the right environment for him. He enjoyed playing trumpet in the school band. He had a group of friends he was close with and a girlfriend who my sisters and I thought was wonderful.

He had never traveled before on his own, and now he was coming to see me. I was proud of my life, and I wanted him to see it. Maybe I could make up for the years I had grown apart from his life. I thought I could provide him a new experience, a different perspective. I had come out to Hawai'i to follow my heart, and I wanted my brother to see that. I was in the midst of my facilitator role, head swimming with the symbols and rituals of rites of passage, and here was my younger brother journeying on his own, stepping out of the confines of his high school life—separated, uninitiated.

"Brahma is a god from the Hindu religion," Daniel finally said. "It's Sanskrit. From the Vedic texts, Brahma, Brahma is God, the creator, the destroyer. He is sort of the source of everything, and everything is an expression of Brahma." We sat down to our breakfast. "Here, this might help. This is a prayer I say silently before every meal I eat. I'll say it aloud this time…

… Brahmārpa'a' brahma havir
brahmāynau brahma'ā hutam

brahmaiva tena gantava'
brahma-karma-samādhinā...[13]

"It translates to this, 'The act of offering is God, the oblation is God. By God, it is offered into the Fire of God. God is that which is to be attained by him who performs action pertaining to God....' It's a powerful concept. It's said to believe the very cosmos evolved out of his being, *Brahma*, and that *atma*, your soul, is the expression of Brahma..." He drifted off, as if he wasn't sure how much more he could really say about this Brahma deity, diving into his own contemplation on the matter.

Taiga came with me everywhere during his visit, a day-to-day in the life of his older brother. He explored the tropical forests, adorned his swim trunks and shades, and rode in the back of my friend's truck up and down the Hilo roads. We drove around the island and saw the sights together, camping at Puna Lu'u beach where the sun set and the full moon rose. He shared about his girlfriend for the first time and how frustrating school was, and how cool he thought my life was. It was the most we had talked, perhaps ever.

"I see," I said, wrinkling my forehead.

"You said you dreamt this," Daniel asked.

"Yes... I was told by an old man to meditate on Brahma." I relayed the rest of my dream to Daniel. We continued with our morning routine in silence, cleaning our camping dishes, packing up our hammocks, scraping the fungus out from between our toes. We reveled in releasing our bodies into the natural world where nothing within sight was human organized, where all was self-organizing.

---

13   A.C. Bhaktivedanta Swami Prahbupāda, *Bhagavad-Gita as It Is* (*The Bhaktivedanta Book Trust International, Inc., August 2012*), 298.

"That's a powerful dream, whatever it means," Daniel finally said.

"Yea," I replied. "I think I'll let it sit for a while."

It was time to hike out of Waimanu back to Waipi'o Valley, back across the threshold river. We were headed back to the long steep road up to the Koa'e kea lookout, where all who traveled to this location could gaze out high above the ocean and just make out the island of Maui, the next island after Hawai'i Island along the Hawai'i archipelago.

The river of Waimanu had grown with rain from the night before. We carried our packs above our heads in waist-deep water, which beckoned us with strong currents to join in its destined journey to the ocean, *kai.* The trail out of the solemn valley was slippery, and we walked cautiously with each step. *Hala* tree seed pods had fallen from the wind, spattering the narrow switchbacks with its paintbrush ends dipped in the mud of the valley.

We walked slowly, tracing our path from whence we came, rewinding, unwinding, and returning.

Clambering out of Waimanu, I turned to look back into the valley to see new waterfalls appear that weren't there before. Water, *wai,* appearing and disappearing, and all life existed in its midst, in its abundance, in its scarcity. Creating, and destroying, it came down from the mountain, the *mauna,* the water collector that traps the clouds that blow in from the ocean.

My brother and I traveled up along the saddle in between the broad active volcano of Mauna Loa, and the steep dormant volcano of Mauna Kea. We were ascending toward a sacred place. I felt wary about approaching. I always did. This volcano was a site where very few people were allowed. Now it is populated with tourists and scientists disturbing the holy peak daily. It did not seem right for me to hurl myself up the side of this mountain. But I wanted my brother to experience it. Perhaps he could feel its sanctity like I could. Perhaps I could show him something he had not yet witnessed, something I desired all to see.

The visitor center was only at nine thousand feet, the peak at nearly fourteen thousand feet. The air was thin and cool. We were sitting at just about the inversion line, a layer of clouds suspended just below us. It looked as if the *mauna* was held afloat on top of the clouds. I pointed beyond the clouds and told my brother to squint his eyes just right to see the vast blue of the ocean thousands of feet below.

We meandered on nearby trails observing the vegetation, what little of it there was. We approached a small garden close by, dedicated to restoring the silversword plant, *āhinahina*, a relative of the pineapple. Their silver color is an adaptation to their cold, high-elevation environment. Tiny, shiny hairs covering the leaves, which are parabolic-shaped, focus warm sun rays on to the plant's growing point in the center, raising the temperature by forty degrees—like a reflector or solar oven.

Āhinahina live for about ten to fifty years as a low, round bush. At the end of their life, they send up a flowering stalk that can grow over six feet tall within a few weeks and produce up to six hundred flower heads. It reminds me of the great pacific octopus who reproduces only once at the end of her life, laying thousands upon thousands of eggs. She spends the last moments of her life guarding her eggs, keeping them hidden and safe.

With a single death comes a multitude of life.

I stared down at the *āhinahina*. What did it really mean to be native to a place? Where was I native to? What specialized adaptations have I evolved to have? If this mountain was thought to be sacred, were the plants and animals that lived on it sacred as well? Were all things that existed sacred because they existed? Was this what Brahma was?

Looking around, I took in the emptiness of vegetation and the scattered life that exists on this barren mountain. I looked over at my brother, who stood with his hands in the pockets of his shorts, wearing my sandals, and had a slouch in his shoulders and bend in his neck as he peered down at the *āhinahina*. I wondered if he was thinking the same as me. I wondered how similar we were as brothers and how different we were as half-brothers. I wondered when I would see him again, if I'd ever move home again where we could grow close during our adult years. Or maybe he would be so inspired by my life he would someday move out here, and we'd live together as brothers, growing food and cultivating our relationship to the land. We would become this place through age and intrigue.

We spent our last day in the Volcanoes National park, where we hiked up to the old remanent crater of Mauna Ulu. He peered down into its depths, still venting steam from cracks beyond our sight.

I thought the week had gone well, save for his complete unwillingness to put sunscreen on his fair skin during the entire trip. He was stubborn like that, hard-headed but strong-minded, with an interest in nearly anything and everything the world of nuance could provide. By the end of the trip, he had turned bright red, burning his body so brutally he broke out in a fever on his plane trip home and missed the whole first week back at school.

Were the actions my brother was making just part of a phase that needed to be outgrown? Was it an adolescent desire to be initiated? Was he self-initiating? Finding his own way to independence? Navigating his own way through the misguided steps of life?

What good had I done for my brother during his week with me? What did he see as he witnessed my life in Hawai'i? What role had I played in his life?

Maybe a week was not enough. I held on to the pains.

We reached the bottom of Waipi'o late in the day. Daniel brought out the sage to complete the circle and we crossed the river, through the threshold, effectively ending the ritual of our valley ceremony. Memories of my brother's trip fluttered into the breeze with a returning flock of egrets flying back into the valley from the open ocean.

Images of Brahma permeated through thoughts of my brother, and my fathers, trying to find meaning, trying to connect it all in an arch of emerging understanding.

Daniel and I reached Koa'e kea as the sun dipped toward the west. The succession of valleys that made up the north side of Kohala was illuminated by the low light. I stared out beyond the valleys and could just make out Maui. I imagined the islands of Kaho'olawe and Lāna'i next to Maui. I pushed beyond to Moloka'i, then O'ahu, Kaua'i, and finally Ni'ihau.

But what lay beyond Ni'ihau?

At that time, Ni'ihau was the last island I knew of that made up the Hawaiian archipelago. It represented the extent of what I knew, the border of my understanding and the limits of who I was. I entered the valley of Waimanu, the oldest part of the youngest island, desiring to find my own passage into adulthood. I emerged with a symbol that would carry me to a place I did not know existed. All the way up the chain to Hōlanikū.

THE ISLAND AND THE CANOE

—

The time had come. I was moving back toward a place that had once freed me of the shackling constraints of society.

The stirred-up water from the freighter's propellers arched a long trail behind us, the last line connecting us to civilization. Honolulu, the tourist mecca of the world, grew smaller with the clouded Ko'olau mountains looming behind, ever promising to cascade rain down upon its inhabitants on the island of O'ahu.

We chugged along slowly. Relief began to settle in as I was liberated by the open ocean. I was on my way back. I was leaving the clustered world of civilization behind.

Underneath Hawai'i Island, the Big Island, lies a geological hot spot forming one of the newest islands on planet Earth, less than half a million years old.[14] O'ahu, however, had once been the center of the world and was the commerce hot spot between the east and the west. Everyone wanted a piece of the pie. It was a gold pot for the hungry nations of power and a melting pot for the people who inevitably came swarming in for economic opportunity, satiating the voracious appetites of exploitative merchants.

I was headed to the oldest of the Hawaiian Islands, thirty million years old: Kure Atoll. Hōlanikū.[15]

I made it through the restless weeks in Honolulu and all our trainings. We gathered six months' worth of supplies, quarantined by freezing and fumigating everything to prevent the introduction of pests or plants to the atoll, and packed it all up in roughly five hundred five-gallon buckets. It was the last stages of preparation that took several weeks, all the while trying to find space to mentally and spiritually prepare for a life of extreme isolation and a drastic shift in living.

Hōlanikū is home to a field camp that can house up to about ten people. Once a US Coast Guard radio station called the USCG LORAN (Long Range Navigation), the concrete facilities were now used as a camp for the Hawaii State Department of Land and Natural Resources, Division

---

14 National Academy of Sciences, *Evolution in Hawaii: A Supplement to 'Teaching About Evolution and the Nature of Science'* (Washington D.C.: The National Academies Press, 2004), 8.

15 Ibid.

of Forestry and Wildlife. The radio tower was taken down, the airstrip runway decommissioned, and a few buildings demolished. But what remained allowed for fairly comfortable living conditions, including a large cistern to catch rainwater, a shed to store a great deal of supplies, a bunkhouse built later by the DLNR to house conservation crew workers, and a spacious main house with multiple rooms, which included a bedroom, kitchen eating area, food storage, and an office-slash-extra bedroom.

We were passengers on a chartered ship for the next week—the time it took to reach our destination of over 1,400 miles away. We had no responsibilities but to make sure we were routinely taking our sea-sick meds. It was a journey across the open ocean and, in some ways, a journey both forward and backward in time.

The morning sunlight rose to meet the downtown skyscrapers, which had all burst out of the ground only within the last half century. Light refracted in a million mirrored directions, illuminating the prosperity and wealth of an economic growth spurt nearly unmatched anywhere else in the world. The nineteenth century marked the beginning of the globalized era, and at the time it seemed all eyes were on the middle of the Pacific Ocean waiting to see what would become of Hawai'i as a nation. Alas, its fate was sealed by the 1893 overthrow of the Hawaiian Kingdom by American insurgents, which eventually led to its illegal and ironic annexation on July 4, 1898, the same day Americans celebrate the US's independence from Great Britain. This was only officially recognized as unlawful nearly a whole century later in 1993 by the US Congress. No reparations whatsoever have been made since. Hawai'i remains a state under the US law, and the Hawai'i sovereignty movement continues to struggle in gaining popular support.[16]

This history is a sad one. This is a nation that fell to the crushing force of western imperialism. Honolulu, the most geographically remote major city in the world, now displays the effects of such history blatantly as it embraces and perpetuates its neo-identity as a tourist paradise, catering first to visitors and raking in their money through the appropriation of Aloha into the industry of hospitality, spurring unsustainable development, which has now spilled over onto the neighboring islands.

I would not miss Honolulu. Being in the city while waiting for our departure was challenging. It was loud and congested. It reminded me of the barrier civilization was for finding the source of my own nature. I didn't think I would find it here, seeing it as only a place I was passing through. It was a means to an end. I was on a mission to find our true source of humanity and I was eager to get out of the city, to be on our way, to sail further and further from that which represented everything I felt was wrong with this world. I had tolerated it for a few weeks, arriving from the more rural and less crowded Hawai'i Island. After each day of preparations, I would go out for a run through the streets. They were dense with traffic and scattered with homeless encampments only one block off of the Waikiki tourist trap strip which gleamed and glistened with utopic perfection.

Perhaps I would miss it after months of seeing only sand dunes and empty horizons of oceans in all directions. I would

---

16 Ku'ualoha Ho'omanawanui, *Voices of Fire: Reweaving the Literary Lei of Pele and Hi'iaka* (Minneapolis: University of Minnesota Press, 2014), 8-25.

miss it after the fourth cycle scouring every last inch of the island—nothing left to explore but the inner workings of my own crazed and isolated mind. I would be fantasizing about Honolulu then and its fascinating lure of people and culture, all finding ways to celebrate the preservation of diversity. I'd miss the idea and freedom of it all, but in that moment, drifting away, I only desired freedom from it.

O'ahu began to fade away and, with it, the constant sounds of a post-industrial world mechanized into a myriad of human labors all working tirelessly to make a living and to keep the economy of modernity progressing toward an endless peak. I had stared out from the stern of this very ship watching the very same island fade away, moving along the exact same destined path toward and beyond Kauai, the last of the inhabited islands of Hawai'i.

The first time already felt so long ago. But the course of our path returned me to those very same sensations.

KAHANA

The M/V Kahana was built in the Gulf of Mexico and designed to be able to traverse shallow waters. By the time it made its way through the Panama Canal and to Hawai'i, the 189-foot-long freighter ship was torn apart and put back together and renamed the M/V Kahana, meaning rebirth. Now its main duties included sending cargo and jet fuel up the chain to Midway Atoll, Kuaihelani, an old Naval station made famous during WWII. Kuaihelani was also rebirthed, turned into a National Wildlife Refuge. It also gets people like us up to the atolls whose job it is to, in a way, rebirth the islands.

Our team of six were bound for Hōlanikū, which sits fifty-five miles northwest of Kuaihelani, the last of the

Hawaiian Islands, barely known to anyone unless they met someone like me who had been there before or someone from the USCG LORAN navigation station that once operated on Hōlanikū. We were more or less dependent on the M/V Kahana, which would travel up to Kuaihelani to drop off all the necessary supplies for the teams of workers and, from there, take the overnight trip to Hōlanikū.

The only practical way teams of conservation workers could get out to Hōlanikū and sustain year-round efforts was through contracted vessels. Without it, the island would suffer. The other permitted vessels that went up and down the archipelago were research vessels, which didn't always have the space nor frequented Hōlanikū as often. Otherwise, there were private flights, but those were also pricey and only got us to Kuaihelani, not to mention they couldn't transport our gear.

It was Hōlanikū's lifeline to civilization. Even as we escaped that very same word, it was the mechanisms of civilization which not only allowed us to be freed from it, but also what allowed a conservation effort for the atoll. We relied on their transportation just as much as they relied on the State of Hawai'i's money. Honolulu, as convoluted as its history is, was the connecting force that tied it all together.

Our conservation crew was made up of workers and volunteers from all backgrounds. Most were locals, but there were also those like me who grew up elsewhere. We had all congregated within the same hull, a sparkle in our eyes, with the ship's crew.

We enjoyed each other's company. I was intrigued by the life underway and the dangers that came with an occupation on the open ocean, and the ship's crew were fascinated by our own team who were crazy enough to go live on a bird colony one quarter the size of central park for half a year. It was a point of interest, an opportunity for conversation out at sea. What kind of person did it take to respond to the ever-changing conditions of the ocean? What kind of person did it take to endure the long, wild, and remote life on an uninhabited island?

It seemed like we were all getting away from something, maybe in an attempt to save ourselves from society or maybe an attempt to save society itself. Maybe it was just me who felt this way. Either way, while underway we all felt the refreshing sense of being rebirthed. We had a new beginning, another chance, another opportunity.

The M/V Kahana dropped us off in the early spring, and if all went well, they'd pick us up in the early fall. We wouldn't see anyone else during that whole time—save the one or two trips of an NOAA research vessel that passed by—and we always looked forward to seeing the M/V Kahana crew's faces again on the other side of the year, six months later. They were the very last faces we saw, still there on that ship, as if they never left, as if they were just out there on the ocean the whole time like immortal seafaring souls waiting to ferry the dead back to the living.

For all intents and purposes, we had departed from the living. For one, because of our severance from society, but also because of the particular geo-mythic positioning of the islands we would be living on.

This was the realm of *pō*.

The shallow-hulled ship continued along, humming and bobbing at a constant ten knots, taking the most direct route to Kuaihelani, which was more or less a straight line that passed a series of islands and atolls between Niʻihau and Hōlanikū.

Atolls are a unique geological feature found within a specific longitudinal band along the Earth. Within this band, the ocean's water temperature is warm enough to sustain a type of coral called hermatypic corals. Created by underwater volcanoes called seamounts, little specs of land eventually grow large enough to break through the ocean's surface, amassing land which creates an island. This process takes millions of years, but once accomplished, the warm-water hermatypic corals can colonize the island just below the surface in the shallow depths where enough sunlight can penetrate the water. These reef-building corals, small sea animals, and plants are actually a combination of two different species working together to create a hard exoskeleton of limestone (calcium carbonate), which eventually forms a protective fringing reef that surrounds the island.[17]

The fringe reef system is one of Earth's most fascinating natural phenomenon. Over millions of years, the volcanic activity of these islands seizes and the landmass poking out of the vast ocean slowly erodes over another millions of years, sinking into the seafloor. This process, called subsidence, is the aging and weathering of the island which is eventually reduced to a merely flattened-top seamount by ocean waves, becoming a guyot. During this stage, the surrounding fringing reef transforms into a barrier reef, one which is further from the shores of the recently formed guyot and forms a deeper lagoon than what once encompassed the island. This barrier reef protects the lagoon from the winds and waves of the open ocean.

The sinking process of subsidence sightly changes the ocean chemistry inside the lagoon. This subtle change has

---

17   "Atoll," National Geographic.

a radical effect on the coral life. Whereas the coral facing outside toward the open ocean remains unaffected by this change, the inside facing coral begins to decay. There are fewer nutrients in the changed chemistry waters, nutrients of which the algae which live within the coral compete for. Fewer nutrients and higher competition mean less opportunity for life, and the vacant coral limestone no longer protected by the scarce algae begins to decay.

This decaying limestone gets broken into pieces by the constant onslaught of ocean waves, churning the limestone into tiny grains of sand. Sand is also formed by a whole ecosystem of invertebrates such as sea urchins, *wana,* and invertebrates such as the parrotfish, *uhu,* who eat the coralline algae, breaking it down into sand particles. Eventually, the processed sand, whether by waves or creatures, are moved by the currents and deposited on the reef, piling up high enough and mixed with other material such as organic matter and seeds that find their way to the same point, forming an island.[18]

We would pass Kaua'i that evening, the last of the main Hawaiian islands. With the setting sun, we were pushing onwards away from the realm of *ao.*

As mentioned in the first chapter, *ao* and *pō* represent day and night, respectfully, and also demarcate several dichotomies that make up our conceptualized world. If day is life, then night is death. There is a story, *mo'olelo,* sometimes referred to in contemporary times as a cosmology, called the Kumulipō. This story is structured as a *mo'okū'auhau,* which is a telling of genealogy tracing all the way back to the creation of the universe. It is a story that once had many

---

18   Ibid.

versions and various lengths and was translated into English by Queen Lili'uokalani while she was imprisoned in her own palace in Honolulu during the overthrow in 1893.[19]

Lili'uokalani ascended the throne in 1891 after her brother David Kalākaua died unexpectedly while acting as the elected king, *mō'ī*, of the Hawaiian kingdom. It was a tumultuous time politically for the nation after efforts by foreigners, *haole,* led by a man named Lorrin Thurston tried to gain power through means of illegal use of smuggled arms and force Kalākaua's hand in 1887 to sign what is known as the Bayonet Constitution. Kalākaua lost all significant power as *mō'ī*, transferring it to the Legislature and Cabinet made up of mostly haole.[20] The movement of *aloha 'āina*, love for the land, although a traditional saying according to Mary Kawena Pukui, was brought forth in the nineteenth century "to rally *Kanaka* nationalism; the *po'e aloha 'āina*, the people who loved the land, were patriots who fought for the *Lāhui*."[21]

However, this expressive movement does not quite translate to the words of nationalism or patriotism. While these English words are used to uphold a people or race, *aloha 'āina* is used to uphold the land. This was a fundamental difference between not just the political forces at play in Hawai'i, but also a collective human orientation to Hawai'i as a place.[22]

Aloha 'āina is still very much alive today as *kanaka māoli* continue to fight for the sovereignty of their *lāhui*.

---

19   Ku'ualoha, *Voices of Fire*, 8-25.

20   Ibid.

21   Ku'ualoha, *Voices of Fire*, 18.

22   Ibid.

Much of Hawaiian knowledge, *ike,* has been preserved through efforts such as Queen Lili'uokulani.

The Kumulipō is made up of sixteen sections called *wā,* divided into two halves which are called *pō* and *aō,* or night and day. *Pō* precedes *aō,* representing the entirety of a divine source of creation where ancestral spirits go after death and are deified as gods. *Aō* is the antithesis of *pō,* a realm entirely compatible with humans and the living. The universe begins with Kumulipō, personified as a male born into the darkness, while Pō'ele is born into darkness as a female. These two are the first and original binary pairs in which all life is a descendant.[23] *Ao* does not come until the second half of the chant after the first seven *wā,* which describes the stages of the world developing and its approach to "light."[24]

The transformation from *pō* to *ao* is a period considered the breaking of light and the dawn of humans. This pinnacle stage explains the flipping of authority from the world of spirits and gods to the realm of humans who took over and dominated. This transformation is what is called *huliau,* meaning overturning or complete change, and is where the first mythical humans appear. Like the early periods of *pō, ao* is also engendered by a pair of manifestations of *pō*: Pōkinikini and Pōhe'enalumamao.[25]

As the M/V Kahana continued its path northwest, we were all, in a sense, moving back in time toward the older and older islands of Hawai'i, one after another, until finally landing at Hōlanikū, the last remaining atoll that still exists above the ocean's surface. It is akin to an astronomer

---

23 Kikiloi, "Kūkulu Manamana," 27-30.

24 Ibid.

25 Ibid.

traveling through space as they peer through their scientific instruments. The further out they gaze toward the edges of the universe, the closer they are to viewing the beginning of time itself, before light and matter existed, the boundary between *ao* and *pō*, the cosmic *hulihia*. So our journey toward *pō*, tracing the Hawaiian island's *mo'okū'auhau*, lay heavy in my mind as I drifted off to sleep to the growing swells of the open cosmic ocean that lay beyond.

NIHOA

I awoke on our first morning underway and rushed outside, knowing we would be approaching the first of the ancients: Nihoa. In the dim light, I could barely make out the tooth-shaped island on the bobbing horizon covered by storm clouds. Nihoa is well known through several different accounts, referenced in multiple chants. It is a mountainous island, with a sheer cliff of nine hundred feet that drops from its highest point all the way to the ocean surface. We won't pass close enough to experience the immensity of this cliff, but I imagine the many seabirds flying around and nesting within the native and endangered *pōpolo* nightshade that grows abundantly on its wide steep slopes and the *loulu* palm down in the crevassed ravines.

The island of Nihoa is inhabited by less common terrestrial species such as the Nihoa finch (*Telespiza ultima*), Nihoa millerbird (*Acrocephalus familiaris*), Brown's amaranth (*Amaranthus brownii*), and Nihoa pritchardia (*Pritchardia remota*), *loulu*).[26] There are also ancient remnants of a human presence—anthropological evidence of agriculture and

26 "Papahānaumokuākea as a Refuge for Rare and Globally Significant Species," Papahanaumokuakea Marine National Monument, July 30, 2020.

altars—all indicating Nihoa, although not valued as a place of wealth for human settlements in the past, was obviously in a valuable location and proximity to the ancient islands further northwest, so many miles away from Lanai'i.[27]

Knowledge has resurfaced, thanks to Kekuewa Kikiloi's archeological and oral-historical work, telling of Nihoa as a kind of base camp to access the next island in line, Moku-manamana, which sits along the path of the sun during its summer solstice procession. Food could be grown on the slopes of Nihoa, providing shelter and sustenance to prepare for the extensive journey out to Mokumanamana. It was an island that became a remote outpost for the recurrent staging and use of the ritual center.

Nihoa demarcates the beginning edge of the Northwestern Hawaiian Islands. The artifactual evidence of people's presence on these islands indicates an occupation that ranged from 1400 AD well into the nineteenth century. The question as to why people would continually venture on long and perilous voyages for their chiefs, or ali'i, struck Kikiloi as a fundamental question worth asking. He suspected it would shed light on the social transformations of Hawai'i and the development of Hawai'i's religious system. Ultimately, perhaps, it could lead a path toward a statehood power system.[28]

By 10:30 a.m. Nihoa was faint in the eastern horizon and soon disappeared below its illusionary edge. I watched a red-tailed tropic bird, koa'e'ula, skim the crest of a swell to our north, joined by two black-footed albatross, ka'upu, who swayed with the wind close to the rolling ocean. As the day progressed, the M/V Kahana steadily made its way toward

27 Kikiloi, "Kūkulu Manamana," 120-155.

28 Kikiloi, "Kūkulu Manamana," 3-22.

Mokumanamana. We passed over a shallow region known as Twin Banks into the Hawai'iloa channel separating Nihoa from Mokumanamana. Spinner dolphins were there to greet us, and we spotted a small group of whales off in the distance. The dolphins emerged at our bow, some breaching the surface as they propelled their torpedo-shaped bodies up into the air. The shallow waters around the Twin Banks—nothing left of these eroded islands except sand bars—were a vibrant yet deep mix of blue colors distinguished from the darker ocean color which surrounded the ship.

Noon came and went. Late afternoon set in with its timeless sensation as the sun appeared to be caught in the western skies. A lone Laysan albatross, *mōlī*, skirted the waves to and fro, either searching for floating food sources or merely exhilarating themself with their tenacious ability to fly so close to the ocean surface without crashing. Multiple red-footed boobies, *'a*, foraged together in the distance, their blue beaks just noticeable enough in the late sun. The day was calm. Most of our crew was relaxing on various levels of the ship. Some made camp on the mid-deck where the warm sun would hit their lounging bodies, all drowsy and inundated with motion sickness meds—our tenacious attempt to keep from plummeting our equilibrium into the unsteady rolling hull of the ship.

I drifted into the swells and currents, trying to ward off my own wavering nausea. I watched the seabirds. I joined the *mōlī* and *'a* above the waves, foraging for ways to accept humanity's evolution not just as mere tragedies, but also as part of some larger purpose playing itself out.

The M/V Kahana was now firmly positioned between the ritual centers of Nihoa and Mokumanamana, two islands that defined the ritual power and religious expansion of

Hawai'i that in part could explain the necessity of centralized social order in the second millennium as populations in Hawai'i expanded.[29] While I stepped on the boat in Honolulu as a means to drive myself away from the residual powers that have emerged into the present day, I now realized I was headed right toward the source of this spark in expansion and growth. Mokumanamana represented what all human populations across the globe struggled with: population expansion. As the civilization grew in size, even out in the middle of the Pacific Ocean of Polynesia, there was no escaping the cultural adaptations that necessitated an evolution in social structures.

I returned my mind to the open ocean, breathing out my spinning thoughts like spinner dolphins departing from their ocean habitat for the briefest of moments. The Hawai'iloa channel would bring strong currents and larger swells, disrupting the already precarious equilibriums of our terrestrial brains. I rested my eyes and worries as we pushed forward.

A SHIP AND HER CREW

Being on a ship on the open ocean provides an opportunity for mingling, which I found very tasteful. A unique bond is created between the ship's manifest (us) and its own crew. The M/V Kahana crew was composed of seven men for this trip: the captain, two shipmates, an engineer, two able-seamen, and the cook. I had learned from one of the able-seamen, a veteran on the M/V Kahana, that there is an important relationship between the wheelhouse where the captain and shipmates function, and the engine room and the deck where the able-seamen and ship engineer function. They always

---

29 Ibid.

have to be communicating, especially the wheelhouse and the engine room, if the ship is to successfully carry out its duty. Also, everyone has a role to play on that ship, none less important than the next. It's a microcosm of society floating on the ocean.

Another morning on the open ocean was spent casting away my thoughts into the wind across the vastness stretching out in all directions. I found the cook outside. Originally from Texas, but now in his older years, he was "a man of the world," having traveled nearly everywhere for work as an executive chef. Before, it was Norway where he met his wife. Now he was on the M/V Kahana. He was sitting out on the deck under the motorboat smoking a cigarette.

"I haven't smoked in years. Quit a long time ago. But I haven't seen my wife in two years, and I can't handle the stress. So back to smoking."

The cook was a little baffled by Virginie's vegan diet—one of the new volunteers for Hōlanikū—but took the news in stride and felt inspired to cook different foods for her. Virginie tried to explain that he needn't do anything special for her, but it was lost in translation somehow. Or I guess cooks are cooks, and if you say you eat a certain way, they're going to take it seriously. It was his job; it was his meaning in life and his contribution to the world.

I walked back to the galley—my sarong wrapped around my legs to protect me from the chill of the early morning. Over the years, I had adopted the use of a sarong, a light piece of cotton common in south pacific cultures that can be adorned in many ways but most commonly like a skirt, which gives it a kind of exotic look if the stereotypically wrong gender wears it as such. The captain, a crude and competent man with a cigar-stained bushy mustache, entered moments later, giving me a look up and down. "What the fuck kind of outfit is that? Are you a Mongolian now with your yurts, or however the hell you say it?" The sleepy galley awoke with an uproar of laughter.

Before, the captain had been chatting about a video he watched recently about yurts being built all over the island of Oʻahu. One of the shipmates chimed in, saying he knew the couple building them. This got the captain going, as any response to his hinted reproach would do.

"Why the hell would anyone want to live in a single circular room like that?" We all took turns illuminating the captain on the true sophistication of the yurt design. It was structurally sound and able to handle high winds, and more spacious and less claustrophobic in a circular room, easy to take down and put back together. I added at the end, "And I think 'yurt' is actually a plural noun. Not sure what a single yurt is called." The captain just cocked his eye at me, then rolled them up and around once to signal he regretted bringing it up.

I grinned and shrugged my shoulders and sat down with everyone else as the laughter from the captain's obscene question settled, proudly still wearing my sarong like a skirt. In a sense, the captain was right to make the connection between sarongs and yurts; they were both examples of efficiency, which came from different cultures and traditions of the world and were adopted in this modern era. He may have not known it, but it was another example of the inner-working success of civilization advancing itself through cultural nuances. It was all tied together—our differences, our tolerances, our sensibilities in an ever-changing, ever-growing humanity.

The engineer was one of those quiet, shy giants. Virginie and I caught him one night sitting alone in the galley waiting for his shift to start. Virginie was editing her photos from the day while I was sifting through thoughts when the engineer came walking in and sat right down in the same chair he always did, the one that faced the clock on the wall.

"The oil ships I work on back in the gulf, man, we neva had so much time to sit around. I ain't got nothing to do on the M/V Kahana but stare at that clock from six to ten. Just staring and staring." Virginie and I perked up from our computers, surprised to hear the engineer talking.

"What was it like on those ships?" I asked, and suddenly, the engineer was firing away about life aboard a different vessel. He had been on an oil transport ship to and from the rigs out in the Gulf of Mexico, working on the clock day in and day out.

"And even then, you neva got good rest, cause there was always somethin' to do. Neva had time to just stare at the clock. Not like this..." he trailed off, staring back up at the clock on the wall. Joe was a man who lived to work.

Joe then screwed up his eyes and looked at Virginie. "So you don't eat meat?" He ended his question with a tone of curiosity and interest. Virginie replied saying she was a vegan. "So what that mean, like you don't eat anything that moves or nothing?"

"No, not technically. I just don't eat animals or animal-derived products."

"No animal products? You mean you don't drink milk, or . . . what else . . . no butta?"

It was completely unheard of to the engineer from Louisiana who seemed to eat nothing but meat. Virginie explained her choice in the matter and the issue with eating animal products. The engineer furrowed his brow, now holding both his elbows with his opposite hands and leaning into Virginie's words.

When she mentioned GMO, he perked up and blurted out, "Oh sure, yeah, I know all about those genetically modified, uh...organs or whateva they called. That stuff is scary what they tryna do to our food. These days you gotta go to a fama's market if you don't want none of that GMO food. Like if they going into our foods and changing them like that, what's it gonna do to our own bodies?"

Virginie and I gave each other a look. It's funny how we all make assumptions about each other. The differences, through time, turn into curiosities, turn into tolerance, turn into learning, adaptation, and growth. These were the gifts of a civilized world, a world we brought with us as we sat late into the night in the swaying galley with the engineer, as we sat with the whole crew eating our nourishing breakfast with my sarong still wrapped around my legs. We traveled together in the M/V Kahana, our canoe, our island, our world.

DEPARTURES AND ARRIVALS

She smiled at me with that big grin she usually hides behind a tough face and gave me that hug she doesn't like giving. I squeezed her through her life jacket and muttered a "see ya later" into her ear, letting her go quick so she could get on with hugging everyone else goodbye.

She stepped onto the inflatable boat and shot two shaka fists up at the sky, motoring away toward the giant National Oceanic and Atmospheric Administration (NOAA) research vessel, the *Oscar Elton Sette*, which could be seen jogging outside the reef, moving back and forth around the atoll. All ships are restricted from anchoring in the surrounding protected waters. Our remaining crew stood on the shore at the water line, waving in return. I turned around and headed up the beach, not wanting to have anything more to do with any kind of prolonged goodbye. We had work to do—a lot of it—and it was going to be that much harder after losing one of our crew members.

"I'm over it," I said coldly to Old Matt, one of the two camp leaders and one of two Matts on the island who we decided to distinguish as Old and Young and as a joke since they were not that different in age and both fairly young. He was standing next to me at the water jugs stationed near the vegetation line. We began lifting our replenished water supply from the *Oscar Elton Sette* into the wheelbarrows, our only mode for transporting supplies around the island.

"Gosh, they're still waving back and forth at each other," Matt said, glancing at the small boat as it continued along the six or so miles out beyond the protective reef. The rest of our crew was still lined up on the shore as if tethered by the fading transport boat.

"Goodbyes aren't a single moment," I started to say aloud to Matt. I lifted one of the large heavy water jugs into the wheelbarrow. "They're like the waning of the moon, just a cycle of phases, the continuity of the present becoming the past." Matt handed me the next jug, giving me a look with those hard-to-read eyes. "I'll still be saying goodbye for a few days, so I don't need to keep saying it here and now," I finished off.

I don't wait for a response from Matt. I grabbed the full wheelbarrow, the sun beating down on my skin glistening with sweat. I dragged it up the beach into our water-storage cove tucked away and protected behind the natural barricade of sand dunes stretching across the entire lagoon-side of the island like a long, curved spine. Those dunes, besides the surrounding emergent reef, were the only thing separating us and our feathered friends from the storms that always threatened from some far away, unknown source.

This day had come as we all knew it would, not an unknown storm but instead the anticipated transition from what had already been a small crew to an even smaller one. It left all of us feeling a bit empty, vulnerable, and uncertain about the days and weeks ahead. Maybe it was just the calm before the storm.

With the summer solstice arriving just around the corner, there was the joy of festive celebration to look forward to. We were now joined by our good friends, Daisy and Nimz, our resident Hawaiian monk seal monitoring team from the National Marine Fisheries Service (NMFS). Although our DLNR team shrunk to five, our Kure family grew to be seven. I was happy to see them, meeting for the second time in a place we all shared a deep love for. But they had come for their own work with the seals, and I knew their festive arrival and the upcoming summer solstice (which Nimz was especially colorful and exuberant about) would be but a blip in an otherwise daunting strategic-work schedule.

* * *

The solstice was a week away. We looked forward to the arrival of the longest day of the year on Hōlanikū. It was an evening of celebration and tradition, and if the winds were low, we'd make a small fire on the beach alongside the shores of the lagoon. We used these fires to burn our seeds collected from the invasive plants. We spent the weeks leading up to the solstice treasure hunting in the field for bits and pieces of marine debris to make costumes out of.

We dressed up in humanity's immortal plastic waste, discarded into the oceans only to wash up resurrected on the Hōlanikū shores. Out here, we danced the discarded dance of humanity's disregard for all other life. We danced the sun away back below the horizon, our costumes made from the undead toothbrushes, lighters, old lobster traps, and abandoned toys spinning alive and rattling together like the skeletal echoes of a primordial past.

It was our ironic way of trying to connect to something eternal. Dressing our bodies with the plastic bits of modern humanity, which had only begun arriving onto the shores of Hōlanikū the last half-century, was our way of celebrating something that had been recognized by humans for eons. But in our way of doing it, all we had to go off of, all we had inherited, were these bits of plastic that would continue to exist long after our bodies would disintegrate into the earth.

The solstice was a celestial event to recognize the eternal inside the temporal, that we live not through our own selfish desires to exist but through our collective desire to live. We desired a shift, but we clung only to what we knew, even when we knew it was the very same thing preventing that shift.

With the arrival of summer, so the spring departed as the sun grew ever-present. As the source for all life begins with the sun, giving off the energy absorbed by the planet and harnessed by its inhabitants, it is also that which takes. The sun took our inviting weather as well, and now with its absence, everything living on Hōlanikū entered into the true test of survival.

The solstice came and went, as did the winds, dying to a near utter stillness. It was all to be expected as the days were becoming longer and the interchange of cool and warm air flowing across the Pacific Ocean was slowing, leaving Hōlanikū with nothing but warm, rising air. This was an El Niño year, warmer currents dominating the Pacific. After what had been a gusting spring with strong cool winds prevailing from the north, as if overnight we awoke to the shock of merciless, thermal heat, which the broad-winged *iwa* birds delighted in congregating along, drafting effortlessly in spiraling masses upward toward the heavens.

The stillness was eerie.

Not only was the ever-present sound of the wind ripping through camp gone, but so was the crashing of the waves against the reef that surrounds the atoll. The lagoon also quieted, becoming a near-perfect reflection of the sky, shining its turquoise color back onto the clouds that hung frozen in the windless heat. If one slipped into the waters at night and lay still as a lotus pad, one could float through the universe, the stars reflecting off its still surface. But soon enough the lagoon of Hōlanikū would start to heat up as well, causing a deep green algae bloom that would turn our shores into a pea soup. No longer would it be a refreshing source to rinse at the end of a long day's work—no longer a pool of stars and galaxies.

As the atoll shifted in feel, sound, and color, so did the smells. Without the wind bringing us fresh air from the ocean, the smell of guano from hundreds of thousands of birds began to permeate through the thickening atmosphere. The stagnation had brought with it another arrival far worse than the stench of bird droppings.

* * *

The shock of the sudden heat triggered a large die-off of birds, notably the albatross populations who build their nests on the ground which heats up quickly during the day. We could spot a dead albatross easily, our eyes so used to the conformed shape of a bird nestled on the ground or pacing across the vegetation with tucked-in wings and bobbing heads. But the lifeless bodies awkwardly slumped over and pressed into the ground disturbingly caught our gaze. We were used to seeing albatross chicks dying, as is the hard and bitter truth of infant mortality across all species, but with the switch of the weather fledglings were all dropping like flies, and with that came the unavoidable signs of death and decay.

The albatross devoted their lives to feeding their offspring, some even giving their life. Even a few of the adults would die as they gave up their food, regurgitating the ocean-foraged resources from their bellies to their chick who waited each day under the oppressive sun. It is the sacrifice that keeps the cycle of existence going. But in that moment, it didn't make it any easier to witness. In fact, watching the departing lives of these dying albatross had prevented me from seeing the opportunity arriving, an opportunity for profoundness I had initially set out to find but had lost sight of and could not see as it stared back at me with open, unblinking eyes.

Many of the species of birds that nest on the Northwestern Hawaiian Islands (NWHI) once populated the main Hawaiian Islands in great numbers, but were decimated by the rapid expanse of humans during the post-European contact era.[30] Now, these *manu* primarily exist within the protected boundaries of Papahānaumokuākea Marine National Monument, established in 2006 (the NWHI have had different levels of protection since 1909). Many of these *manu* colonies were threatened into becoming extant by past and even present human actions. Today, the populations are recovering thanks to conservation efforts.

The beginning of the windless heat coincided with the annual albatross count. Every December, the newly laid eggs were counted and recorded by the winter crew. The summer crew then returned for a count right before fledging season to get an accurate read on the reproductive success and population growth of the three species of albatross on the island. This is but one data point used by the State of Hawaii Department of Land and Natural Resources (DLNR), Division of Forestry and Wildlife (DOFAW) that measures whether the restoration efforts have been effective.

It is a big deal, one enjoyed for its recent positive count results, as well as a welcomed relief from the otherwise arduous invasive plant removal constituting up to 75 to 80 percent of the work, being the highest impact on restoring the natural nesting habitat of the eighteen species of seabirds. This season would prove to be challenging.

We immediately began falling behind schedule, unable to keep up with the life cycle growth of *Verbesina encelioides*, which is rated as one of the most invasive of all the plants on Hōlanikū. A member of the aster family, this sunflower native to the American Southwest regions of the US, was

---

30   David Cameron Duffy, "Changing Seabird Management in Hawai'i: from Exploitation through Management to Restoration," *Waterbirds* 33, no. 2 (1 June 2010): 193-207.

perfectly adapted to wreak havoc on the open, bare ground of the island after the USCG station was removed in 1994. It grows very quickly, forms dense stands, and outcompetes low-growing native plants that provide essential habitat for nesting seabirds.

We traded out our spray packs for our spray cans of non-toxic paint used to mark the ground next to each and every albatross chick to avoid double counting. We distributed our tally counters and prepared for what would inevitably be a major setback in our treatment cycle. There was no good way to go about it. It was ideal to count the chicks as late into the season as possible to get an accurate read on the reproductive success rate, but this just so happened to be right when the *Verbesina* started to really take off in growth, triggered by the increased rays of sunlight and overall heat. Covering an area of one hundred eighty-eight acres may not sound like much, but a team of only five attempting to count what would amount to nearly twenty thousand individual fledglings was no small feat.

The five of us took off in separate directions, assigned to different sections of the island divided more or less equally among us not just by size, but also the difficulty of the terrain. The goal was to get the count done in a week—an ambitious goal. We had a late start on the first day, gathering all of our equipment, going over the game plan, and training the volunteers. In the late morning, it was already the hottest temperature on record of the season thus far, 85 to 89 degrees Fahrenheit. The high summer humidity, measured as heat index, made the temperatures feel even oppressive, upward to one hundred degrees.

I dragged my feet out to my section, starting to forget what this work was all for. I felt stuck on only the flower, not respecting the path that precedes the blooming. Thoughts ruminated as I began my count. With each click of the counter, I weaved through clusters of albatross chicks scattered across the island minute by minute, hour by hour, rumination by rumination.

The day ended but doubt lingered in the air. I grew quiet that evening, turning inward and isolating myself with the hollow feeling growing in my gut. I wanted to focus on the albatross count, on our work, on this island and its magic, and appreciate the fact I got to be out here a second time. But instead, I could only feel my hands clenching into fists and my teeth biting into regret. It left a bad taste in my mouth I couldn't get rid of. It stuck around, fowling my breath, and with each exhale it began to pour out around me.

What was I really doing here? The question held on tight like the months of sweat staining in my clothes.

It is often an area of contention to try and find the common ground between preserving old ways and progressing into new ones. Understanding a healthy future of our relationship to the environment will require us to see beyond short-term changes and be a part of the greater forces binding us to place as we are intricately connected to each other through all lifeforms that share these lands and oceans through time.

I was stuck. All I saw was how tired I was growing, how small our team was, and how little power I had to do anything about it. I grew irritated, wanting to take out my own shortcomings on anything and everything.

I waited impatiently for emails from my family and friends, and when they didn't arrive, I took it out on them for being too self-absorbed in their own lives. When I collapsed yet another wedge-tailed shearwater, 'ua'u kani, burrow in the field by walking over it in my heavy boots, I took it out on the *naupaka's* uncooperative twisting growth form tripping me any chance it could get. When the volunteer crew member, Virginie, busied around proactively from one project to the next as I lay incapacitated on my bed, tired and defeated after our first day of bird counting, I took it out on her seeming inability to relax and give it a rest. It was all building into a ridiculous form of self-loathing.

It caused me to run, to get away from the others so I wouldn't inflict my nastiness on them. But even so, it still slipped out. I abruptly told Steph, a volunteer from New Jersey, after dinner how she always finished other people's sentences for them, and she immediately apologized saying, "Oh god, do I really do that? That must be so annoying!" I realized what I just did and tried to remedy the situation by telling her I didn't think it was annoying. In fact, someone can't be annoying, only annoyed, and if I was annoyed by this, it would be a problem I have, not her. Confusing her, I walked away and left her scrubbing dishes alone, leaving me annoyed with myself and determined not to see what was truly bothering me, determined not to confront the death piling up on the island.

* * *

The week pressed on, pushing our limits as the temperatures continued to rise and testing our sanity. We were all enduring it, but each in our own sufferable way. Each day began with less enthusiasm than the next, less chatter during breakfast, less briefing on the day's plan. We all knew the drill at this point: get back out there from where you left off and start counting. There was no need to waste a single breath reiterating it. We'd need each and every ounce and gram and droplet and calorie of effort back out in the field. We put our heads down and marched back out, each in our own direction. Each in our own world.

My fiery emotions, which sparked at the beginning of the week, had settled into a numbing headache. I was beginning to pay the price for my hot-headedness, the residual effects piling on top of each other with every passing day. I shuffled out to my counting zone, beginning a new section known for getting easily turned around in, with mature *naupaka* bushes growing thick along the wave of dunes that all looked the same. It was a zone with few albatross because of how dense the vegetation was; any chicks hatched in here have already scuttled their way out to a more open area where they would eventually spread their wings and take flight, but we try to start the count before the chicks start to move.

I was hardly aware I had departed camp. I had given up my feverish pursuit in victim-blaming, too tired to keep up the burgeoning work it took to maintain such lavishly sour convictions.

Instead, I had gone into a complete state of denial. I didn't realize I was becoming increasingly dehydrated. I just wanted it to be over. I just wanted to get back to the plant treatment cycle. I forced my way through the *naupaka* snagging at my clothes, threatening to trap me with every thrust of my limbs. I paced on the open makeshift trails to find new entry points into the thicket, possible areas I had missed. I kicked sand unnecessarily with my hot boots while knowing I'd have to use more energy clamoring about in places in which, even though there were most likely no birds, it was important I still checked because covering the entire island was the only way to show distribution and abundance.

I would not make it through the whole day.

I stumbled back into camp where the crew was already taking their lunch break. Without a word, I stood in front of the little swinging gate to the main building we built to prevent the Laysan ducks from sneaking inside. I must not have looked right. Everyone looked up slowly from their lunch which was last night's leftovers. They stared at me like I was some drunken bad cowboy swaying in the entrance of a saloon. Beads of sweat rolled down my pale skin. My eyesight turned blurry as I shuffled in and sat down in the empty seat, grabbing something that resembled food. I started chewing it.

My head began pounding. My stomach grew nauseous.

Everyone waited for me to say something. Nothing moved past my chapped lips except shallow breaths.

"You don't look too good," Naomi, one of the camp leaders, finally said, slicing the silence I brought in with me.

"Yeah," I managed to gurgle. "I think I'm done."

I dropped the food, raised my failing body off of the chair, and headed back outside toward my bunk room, my prison cell of pain and torture for the next little while.

I threw up as soon as I was out of sight, behind the bunkhouse. I crawled to the floor of my room with an ice pack around my neck and a thermometer under my tongue, where I promptly lay for hours spinning and falling in delusion while the rest of the crew strapped on their gear and persevered into the scorching afternoon sun.

I had lost the reins. All manner of images and thoughts, voices, and sound came crashing together like a symphony out of tune and sync. Succinct time became extinct with nothing to fill its absence but chaos. I had succumbed to the growing self-inflicted pressure to achieve our primary objectives. I had been bent and pried open by a flurry of my own wishes that my work was somehow more than this. I was out here, alone with my team and away from the rest of the world, in a place protected from the world, holding on to some imagined deeper purpose to bring these islands to others, to share the wonderful relationship we could all have to a place as precious as Hōlanikū. But I was failing in our most immediate needs as a habitat technician. Now we would all pay the price. Our team shrunk once again. I had been decommissioned.

I awoke from my episode of heat exhaustion on the floor of my bedroom with a thawed ice pack lying limply in a puddle of water by my head. My bones ached, but the pounding in my head was gone, and it seemed my stomach had finished its bout of turmoil. It was only then I became aware of a crackling on the two-way radio in the center room of the bunkhouse.

"Main house to bunkhouse, do you copy? Jon-Erik, you awake? You okay, buddy? What's your temperature? Dinner's ready if you're hungry. Over."

The sun had departed behind the dunes bringing with it the arrival of the evening, a time in which all creatures on Hōlanikū this time of year, including seven humans, looked forward to. I raised myself onto my hands and knees and crawled over to the window. The whole crew was sitting out on the picnic table already with plates full of food. I smiled, for what felt like the first time all week, seeing them all together like that.

It was a challenge for the camp leaders to figure out how to balance the needs of the team and the demands of the atoll. Hōlanikū required the leaders to always be adjusting their objectives and goals as one could always bet some new unexpected event would turn up. It was perhaps the hardest part about managing a crew on the atoll. There were priorities out here, priorities that needed our constant attention, but the priority of our health and well-being always remained the highest. I knew this. I was not a newcomer to atoll, having been out here prior in 2015. I knew better; it was my responsibility to know better. We had been trained for this, trained on how to pace ourselves and taught about dehydration and how to avoid it. I took pride in my sensibilities and attuned monitoring of my health. But I also took pride in my hard work, a little too much pride. It got the better of me, overriding my need to take care of myself. Instead of showing my vulnerabilities to the others and expressing my need to rest and recuperate, to share during our weekly check-ins what was going through my mind, body, and soul, I had hidden the signs even from myself.

Out in such an extremely remote field camp, it was of utmost importance we check in with ourselves. There is only so much another person can tell from their perspective on how someone else is feeling, and often the signs something is wrong are not easy to see until it is too late. The team leaders were well-trained in spotting signs, but the danger of my situation was I was very good at hiding it. The consequences of me losing my sense could have been dire for the program. A medical evacuation in such a remote place could affect future camps due to safety concerns brought to light from an incident or situation.

The smell of bird guano and death was still ever-present, but somehow it didn't smell so bad anymore. Just as I was heading down the steps of the bunkhouse to join everyone for dinner, I noticed the lonesome fresh body of an adult Laysan albatross, *mōlī,* lying still as the windless air, its neck and head resting upon the recently hot, now cooling sand.

I stopped and stared, examining the once-living *mōlī*. It wasn't there in the morning when we all got up with the rising sun, and it wasn't there when I had retreated to the bowels of my room under the heat of the zenith sun. It must have only just died at some point when I was lying helplessly on my back.

"I copy. I'll be on my way."

I studied the lifeless *mōlī*. How large of a bird, yet how small and light and fragile it had become in death. I just stood and watched the *mōlī*. I watched its stillness. I watched its presence. I watched its absence.

Within Hawaiian epistemology exists the concept of *mana*, a term which has been appropriated and borrowed by many to mean something like the energy contained within any corpus or contained mass. *Mana*, how I have come to interpret it, means "power" or "authority."[31] It is a force one inherits, a recognition that extends to all life and even any mass or form, such as a rock or a river. This perspective helps us to understand what is central about the relationship between humans and all other life. Connecting our lives with the very *mana* of the birds brings forth human significance in the context of a world we share with other life forms. Without that context, our reason or purpose for existing is left shrouded in a dichotomous mystery of separated forms—us and them. Instead, we ask, who is the albatross to us? Who are we to the albatross? Who are we together?

All of this I had begun learning before setting out to Hōlanikū a second time, and all of it I could no longer see during our most trying times. How easy it can be forgotten when faced with despair, when shrouded in helplessness

---

31   Kikiloi, "Kūkulu Manamana," 303.

pressing down on my heart through the heat and suffering of life I was out here to help save. I was falling into the same issue all of humanity had been struggling with for centuries now: losing the connection to the practices which bind us to our own humanity—the humanity that leaves in its path the riches of life, actually living life, blooming with diversity. That we, for all that being alive is worth, can cultivate greater and greater biodiversity.

I looked down at the bird whose life was no longer with us, but perhaps whose *mana* I could still preserve and righteously transfer into my own personal process of ritual practice. I forgave the world for leaving us without enough resources to do our job well. I forgave myself for forgetting why I was out here. I began to also listen to these *manu* enacting their lives over and over again, from one generation to the next.

We would continue to press ahead into the weeks before us, and we would continue to struggle uphill, and the albatross would indeed continue to die. But now I saw them, and I saw in them the opportunity that arrived through their own departure from this world. I was a habitat restoration technician, but with that role, there was a chance to focus on sharing something beautiful and meaningful with people back home who awaited knowingly or unknowingly to be reunited to a relationship with the *manu.*

FLEDGLING SEASON

Every time I turn my head, I see yet another young albatross run into the direction of the wind, their wings flapping as hard as they can muster, catching flight at the moment of full commitment and lifting into *lani,* the sky, the heavens.

The island abounds with the plethoric energy of albatross fledglings. The time has come for these birds of the ocean to embark on their next phase of life, to charge ahead with nothing but a compelling instinct and an empty stomach into the vastness of the unknown, to wander the ocean as a forager in solitude.

This is the nature of the albatross—a nature guided by millions of years selecting for behavioral instincts that promote the survival of this species. In order to survive, the albatross must transform from a vulnerable dependent chick who relies on their parents for warmth, shade, and food into an independent adult who can fly, forage, and reproduce. To fully become an adult albatross, however, the chick enters an in-between stage as a fledgling and eventually will become a juvenile.

I came out to Hōlanikū not as a trained biologist with any expertise in the natural sciences, but as a volunteer and worker, curious and fascinated by a distant and remote part of the Earth. My understanding of ecology and the various species on this atoll was limited. I came to step away from the world shown to me by others, to understand my own story and, through this, the story of all life.

I came to seek an understanding of the patterns of the universe. For some reason, this particular species of bird, the Laysan albatross, the *mōlī*, had much to tell me on the universal pattern of leaving and returning home.

* * *

When evening comes and we all put down our work tools and shed our sweaty, sticky work attire, we fill our bellies with the rationed nourishment we brought with us from civilization. We then head out to the heart of the atoll—the lagoon—to watch a few more fledglings disappear beyond the reef, beyond the horizon, where the sun will faithfully set.

By now, we had spent more time on this island than we had remaining. We were fully adjusted and integrated into the daily routine of our lives along with the lives of our fellow bird inhabitants. It was no longer surprising to hear the harsh screech of a red-tailed tropicbird, *koa'e'ula*, as we stepped a little too close to their nesting ground. The fluttering of multiple white terns, *manu o kū*, around our heads as we maneuvered through the carcass of an old dead beach heliotrope tree no longer triggered emotional awe but, rather, was duly noted and slipped into our peripheral experience as we focused on the laborious and primary tasks at hand.

We moved without thought, like seasoned skiers across the mogul-like topography of burrows stretching throughout the island's sandy-soil earth. The stink of our clothes and algae water-logged skin was no longer noticeable. The periodic sharp sting of the paper wasp nor the throbbing of a tick bite caused alarm. The wailing of the wedge-tailed shearwater, *'ua'u kani*, the glottal croak of the brown noddys, *Noio koha,* nesting, or even the dramatic hissing and rasping of the territorial Laysan ducks right outside our windows had replaced the white noise of the car traffic we used to fall asleep to in the city.

We were now fully accustomed to Hōlanikū. Our habits, our routine, and our way of life now integrated into the sounds, sights, smells, and feelings of this strange world. The world of humans was now the land of the strange, and upon our return, we would be the strangers.

Humans are particularly adept at adaptation. It is central to our story as humans, as it is for nearly all life. To survive in the world, we must adapt to that world. As newborns, we are protected and cared for. It is that temporary state of dependency and vulnerability we call home, one that lasts a relatively long time for humans, but eventually and inevitably fades into our subconscious as we mature and grow into full consciousness. Home, no longer a state of being, blooms into a concept we hold on to as the world reveals itself more fully.

I cannot help but think of home while I watch these albatross take flight and leave this island. That place of home, that notion, that feeling residing in all of us is where we come from. It is the resting place, the place that nourished us, raised us, and comforted us. But it can also be that place that deserted us, neglected us, abused us, and threatened us.

Home is not a perfect place, and this is all too true for the albatross. I was living on an island that serves as the breeding and nesting ground for hundreds of thousands of birds. It is their home, their sanctuary, a place hidden from most of the world and most of the dangers, which allows a small representation of these various species to perpetuate their existence. But the island itself is also home to dangers that, when encountered, could end the life of one of these birds just as easily as the dangers residing outside the island. Ultimately, their home is the greatest threat to a chick's survival. If the chick is not able to leave the island, it will surely perish.

The ability to adapt is the ability to embrace the changes that come our way, to somehow be prepared for that which has yet to come: the unknown. Yet, somehow incorporated into our very being, we are equipped with a preparedness to face a world full of the unexpected. The young albatross, although never faced with the experience of flight themselves, are equipped with the instinctual response to the wind. They know the wind, even upon meeting it for the first time. It is the wind that takes them far, far from home.

We humans took a different evolutionary path. We created society.

Another way of looking at domestication and the human tendency to cling to the "home" state is to see it as the prolonging of adolescence. Adolescence is a period of risk-taking, much of which is dictated by the developmental state of the brain. Teenagers, and those well into their twenties, are radical by nature—willing and able to explore new ideas and take substantial efforts toward the manifestation of those actions. Our species' valuing of such juvenile traits from an early evolutionary period has enabled us to excel in the world in a way unmatched by any other animal.

Even as humans have evolved to extend the period of childhood and adolescence in development, it does not mean they do not still have to mature into the same adult state in which all other animals do. We are bound to the same archaic patterns, regardless of how greatly our modern lives deviate from nature. It also seems with the ability to prolong childhood comes the risk of individuals never actually making it into the psychological transformation of adulthood.

When my brother died, I wanted to make meaning of it. I wanted to understand. I held on to the idea something caused him to drown, that it could have been prevented. I needed to make meaning of it. Maybe it was a way of coping, to make sense of something beyond my reach or control. If I couldn't make meaning of it, then I couldn't move through it.

No one can see beyond a choice they do not understand.

Between my two seasons of work on Hōlanikū, I lived on an old macadamia farm with my good friend Taapai. We lived in rustic tents, *hale,* on the hill of the orchard. Taapai was a beautiful gardener, collecting so many plants that when it came time for him to move up the Hamakua coast, he had but only a few belongings beyond his multiple truckloads of plants.

Near his garden of plants, he had pounded two tall posts into the ground. I found Taapai on a particularly clear night when the stars revealed their distant presence to us. He was sitting with his poles, which were like the two masts of a voyaging canoe, a *wa'a.* He had put the poles in the ground when he first moved onto this property. When I asked him what they were for, he said they were so he could orient himself to this new place.

"They are in a line. This one in front of me points to the east, and this one points to the west. Now I know where I am in space, and in time," he explained as he looked up in the night sky to see where the constellations fell.

I held on to that lesson when I returned to Hōlanikū. I wanted to make sure I was not just drifting through life, but that I had aim. To have aim, one must know what to aim at and, more importantly, where to aim. Otherwise, we not only risk always missing the mark, but we may eventually lose our way.

Overvaluing juvenile traits has created its own problems, problems we see every day in society. This problem has evolved alongside the adaptations that have come with human domestication, and cultures around the world have prescribed essential developmental pathways to ensure the values of adulthood are preserved and perpetuated as well. The human, like the albatross, must still leave its proverbial home.

Either way, that place of home occupies a space in our mind, a domain that holds many things congruent with our life's journey. Even as we must leave home, we also must return, no matter how far and wide we travel. No matter how long we wander upon the vast oceanscape, foraging food for our soul, the home of our psyche beckons and awaits our return. Everything, eventually, returns to its source.

* * *

Light split across the eastern horizon and spread out over the sky. A gentle and steady morning wind pushed against my body, pulling the rising sun into the day. I began my dance on the rooftop of the main house, standing what felt like high above the island.

I danced "Ke Ha'a La Puna," a song, *mele*, from the Hula Pele tradition, a *mele* that comes from the Pele and Hi'iakaika-poliopele story, *mo'olelo*. I had just begun learning the ritual of *hula* before I decided it was time to return to Hōlanikū. I was awkward at it and had only really learned the one dance, but I knew it all the way through. I knew it well enough to get up each morning and practice before work.

When we first arrived, the adult albatross were still plentiful. I would stand on the roof with the wind and dance among the many pairs of albatross mates as they danced their own ritual. Albatross are known for their showy dances, used for mating. Sometimes two or three birds would congregate, facing inward toward each other, and proceed through a series of moves that can really only be described as dancing. They would flick their wings out and bend their necks back into it so that their beaks would land in the open space between their bodies and the wings, a kind of mock preening. Then they might bob their heads up and down in a wave-like pattern or shake their heads back and forth in rapid succession while whistling a wailed shrill. After that, they would point their beaks to the sky, lift up on their three webbed toes, and let out a single cooing note to the heavens, *lani*. If done right, it seemed, they would dance in sync. Now that most of the chicks had grown up into fledglings, the adults had returned to the open ocean, free from their duties as parents. The island was much quieter, without their dancing.

It was even a bit lonesome. A few adult albatross arrived to feed their chicks, but with each passing day, their presence became rarer and rarer. I remained. I danced alone. I danced to a song that describes one of Pele's favorite places to go and relax by the water: Ha'ena, in the Puna district of Hawai'i Island. I danced about a place Pele calls home. I danced a song which sings of home, carrying in my movements a place as beautiful as the words in the song.

I cannot say how my fellow Kureans carried home with them while out on Hōlanikū. But I could watch how they carried themselves out there upon the sensuous world of Hōlanikū, and maybe that was the same. I could see how they, like me, responded to the prophetic event of every single albatross fledgling reacting to a large squall passing over, how they cast their wings out to catch the wind to feel the force lift their bodies into the destiny they were meant to live out. I saw how we all stopped whatever it was we were doing, our human task instantly becoming purposeless compared to the purposeful drive of these young albatross attempting first flight. They ripped our attention away from our human constructs; they called to our souls' yearning to be filled with as clear a purpose as these *manu*.

For the birds, the wind brought with it something far more seductive than a mere sense of home. We carry our home with us, but the wind carries us beyond what we could ever imagine. The thrill, the wonder of a world beyond our reckoning, calling us forth into unimagined experiences of fate and destiny.

When the squall would pass over and the winds would die down, we would be broken from the spell like being awoken from a dream. The albatross fledglings calmed back down, returning to whatever they were doing before—preening their feathers, smelling the air, stretching their feet, waiting to grow just a little more. We drifted back into ourselves, our souls slipping back into the confined space of our human psyche, turning once again to our conservation duties so that these birds and the many generations of birds to come may experience this world we are all mysteriously brought into.

* * *

Our lives on Hōlanikū had shaped and molded into routines befitting to our character, suitable to our present needs. The lives of us few that lived together in such close and lengthy proximity were encased in the boundaries of the conditions of this island. Yet we each lived separately in our own paradigms, each of us responding differently to this isolated wildlife sanctuary, each of us yearning to obtain some kind of transformation. Some kind of change from what we were before we set out on this sojourn of seasonal work. Hoping for growth. Hoping to gain something. Hoping to become something.

As the island slowly became our whole world and the whole world slowly became but a distant glimmer on the horizon, we woke up each day and decided what it was that defined us, here and now. We decided what we would bring with us from our past into this new and different world, and what we would lay to rest.

When I would wake up each day and watch the lives of the myriad of birds I was immersed in constantly, I could not help but feel a kind of separation. I was in their home and separated from my own. It was an uncomfortable feeling, but it was one I had become used to, and like the fledgling albatross, it was a feeling I learned to lean into, a feeling that was a guiding instinct toward growth and perhaps, ultimately, success.

I wonder if my brother ever felt the same connection, or disconnection. Did he and his friends venture into an unknown territory of thought? Did they dream of the world being different, did they dream of a different world beyond what they knew, beyond home? I wonder what my brother thought of when he thought of home. Did he get enough time in his short life to leave home—to see it from the outside—to look back at it and appreciate even the frustrations that stacked up as he battled for his will to be free from society?

We all carry with us our own idea of home. I think of a great many things. I think of a city smoothed between mountains and sea, saturated with moisture, and brimming with tall, thickly barked Western hemlocks and Douglas firs. I think of my three older and uniquely different, yet quintessentially the same, sisters telling me how cute I am but also how stubborn I can be. I think of my younger, yet growing up faster than me, brother and the room we used to share when I had short straight hair and he had long golden locks. I think of my mom in a denim jacket and Ray-Ban sunglasses driving a Land Cruiser in the mountains with Mazzy Star playing on the stereo. I think of my father in a polo shirt with a big grin on his bright face like he's the luckiest dad in the world. I think of my stepfather with long hair younger than I am now with all four of us kids holding his two hands, taking turns riding on his shoulders through town to get pizza.

I think of what once was, and I cling to the memories of those once-upon-a-times, fearing that if I let go, I somehow will no longer know who or what I am. I will no longer know where I came from or where I am going.

To know where we are going, we must also know where we came from.

There are some behaviors in nature that are truly miraculous, and the navigating abilities of the albatross are no exception. Once an albatross fledgling successfully takes off in flight, it roams the oceans for upward of three to six years. It is almost an impossible amount of time to grasp. Then, after those years of solitude wandering across thousands of miles of open blue, the albatross makes their way back to the island and their colony from which they originated. The returning albatross can find its exact nesting site from all those years before.

Do the albatross cling to those memories of those once-upon-a-times? Do they sense an urge to return to their own place of origin? What is the felt experience of the albatross as it finally lands on the shores of their home, now as a full-fledged adult? Do they know a transformation has occurred?

Do some lose their way? Do some never make it back?

To understand is to choose to go beyond where one can see.

DEATH OF OUR LIVES

The sun was already shining brightly in the sky as I walked the path to the main house on a Saturday morning, passing by the white terns, *manu o kū*, and brown noddies, *noio kōhā*, nesting on corners of the concrete buildings. I was headed to the kitchen to make a cup of coffee, but as I looked around something caught my eye.

I made this walk to the main house every morning, waking up in the bunkhouse and shuffling over to have breakfast and coffee. I would walk the sixty seconds it took, glancing around to see familiar sights and sounds. It was always the usual scene: The same *mōlī* chicks lying about or busy cleaning their feathers and picking out their down, *'a* gathering nesting material and croaking at each other, *mōlī* adults swooping low, banking across the air to find a place to land and feed their chicks.

Bound to a tiny island filled to the brim with wildlife, we would look at everything, all the time. We never missed a beat. The island became like the back of our hands, a kind of intimacy with the land hard to match anywhere else. Or, at least, a kind of relationship to the land found rare these days. Our lives were swept up by the details of this small landmass. There was change occurring constantly, sometimes gradually, sometimes abruptly. We didn't just notice these occurrences. They affected us. Absent from the modern commercial world competing to capture our attention, we were captured solely by the imagery of this place. Our mood blended with the mood of the island, and it could change as quickly as the weather.

I noticed there was something different moving around. So had Old Matt, one of the camp leaders who was already on the front concrete slab of the main house, his hair sticking straight up as it did in the morning after running his fingers through it to shake out the sleep. He, too, was looking across the field in front of our camp, marked with scattered patches of *kawelu* grasses. Darting from patch to patch was a trail of tiny yellow-flecked bodies of fluff.

Some of the most dramatic work done out here on Hōlanikū can be attributed to the introduced Laysan duck, *Anas laysanensis*, a critically endangered species of waterfowl endemic to the Northwestern Hawaiian Islands (NWHI). In 2014, a group of Laysan ducks was collected from Kuaihelani to become the founding population on Hōlanikū as an attempt to spread the Laysan duck to more islands to buffer the species' existence in case the population crashes on one of the two other islands where there are wild populations.

This waterfowl originated from Laysan Island, Kamole, further down the chain of NWHI. Kamole is unique among the Hawaiian Islands due to it having a large, shallow, hyper-saline lake in the middle, which the Laysan ducks forage for aquatic invertebrates, terrestrial arthropods, seeds, algae, and succulent vegetation.[32] The entire species existed solely on Kamole for one hundred fifty years before concerns about its extinction led to a translocation program to Kuaihelani, where there is now an established population. From there, Hōlanikū was selected to expand the population because, like Kuaihelani, there is a year-round human presence that can monitor the ducks, as well as fresh-water seeps, foraging habitat, no predators, and protective dunes.

"You see any hens with the ducklings?" Matt asked, crouching down to get a better angle as the sun pressed into our gaze. I looked around, forgetting all about my morning routine in search of coffee and breakfast. Our routines were always broken up like this. That was the routine—constantly looking, sensing. It wasn't just a full-time job. It was a way of life out here.

I couldn't see an adult, which meant both Matt and I fell silent and began to listen. First, I could only hear the distant sounds of the sooty tern, 'ewa'ewa, colony toward the eastern side of the island, and beyond that the ever-present low rumbling of ocean waves breaking across the atoll's emergent reef. But then came the soft chirp that could only be a hen calling for her ducklings.

The summer crew gets to monitor the breeding season. We would head out daily to check the seeps, various fresh-water sources around the island created specifically for the

---

32   J. Fischer and D.B Lindenmayer, "An Assessment of the Published Results of Animal Relocations," *Biological Conservation* 96 no. 1 (November 2000): 1–11.

ducks, to figure out the latest state of the broods. It began as an exciting and pleasurable experience—hens with five to seven little ducklings running amuck—but the cuteness wore off quickly. Those ducklings and inexperienced hens would do a less than optimal job keeping track of each other, and if a hen lost her ducklings and did not find them, they would not make it. Young, downy ducklings have difficulty with thermoregulation. As the ducklings get older, they can be more independent, but until then they must rely on the hen to keep them warm in the colder weather or after a day of swimming in the seeps.

Every day, the number of ducklings with each hen changed. Sometimes she had less, sometimes more. The ducklings were constantly mixing up which hen was their mother. We occasionally found a stranded duckling who would sometimes reunite on their own or join a different brood. We would avoid intervening in this process since contact with humans causes stress, but if the situation called for it, we would reunite hens with their ducklings, which proved to be fruitful. After crawling through *naupaka* and sidestepping around burrows for eight hours a day, we would return out into the field to search for where those missing ducklings might be. Old Matt called it "Ducks of Our Lives," like some soap opera. The problem was we were pretty useless at changing the behavior of the new mother hens who did not have the experience to keep her ducks in a row, so to speak. Even when a duckling would be reunited with a brood, the same inexperienced moms would go right back to losing their ducklings day in and day out.

As Old Matt crouched and I stood in suspense, I let out a sigh of relief when the ducklings also heard their parent's call, running in the direction of the adult, and the brood reunited.

Old Matt stood up slowly and gritted his teeth slightly, sore from a week of restoration work, and raised his arms high up in the sky, stretching and letting out his own big sigh.

"Never a dull moment on Kure! Coffee?"

Our impromptu weekend Laysan duck monitoring session luckily turned out okay. We were able to identify which adult it was by the alphanumeric and color-coded plastic band on her leg and counting how many ducklings she had, updating our monitoring log before going about our casual day off. But this would not always be the case. As more and more chicks would hatch and broods would form, our days of stretching and relaxing on a Saturday morning would become less common.

The amount of effort it took to monitor the Laysan ducks was enormous. Wildlife reintroduction programs maintain a low success rate. A study from 2000 estimated the success rate over time of 116 reintroduction programs around the world was between 26 percent and 32 percent.[33] Another survey from 2014 looked at the approaches used in these programs, identifying an emphasis on improving biological knowledge as an avenue toward greater success.[34]

The 2014 survey suggested an alternative approach to improve the success rate of such programs might lie in the human dimension, "specifically, the types of leadership and styles of management under which reintroduction programs are operated."[35] Our team's effort fell into this approach,

---

33 Ibid.

34 Alexandra E. Sutton and Roel Lopez, "Findings from a Survey of Wildlife Reintroduction Practitioners," *F1000Research* 3, no. 29 (January 29, 2014): 1-2.

35 Ibid.

using an adaptive management strategy in which as we monitored and documented activities, we occasionally changed them accordingly while also consulting with experts. We worked together as best we could, allowing time at the end of each day for the duck monitoring. We would try to end our primary objectives early to accommodate, but sometimes it ended up taking more time than we had anticipated.

Life on Hōlanikū is a continuum of call and response. We see the changes and respond to them. It is a lifestyle and mode of work that requires a continuous relationship with the environment. Hōlanikū is fortunate, in a way, because there is a constant presence of habitat restoration technicians and biologists and it is a relatively small area, so workers can become very intimate with the island ecology. The managers hold a particularly special relationship to the atoll since they return every year, becoming so closely connected to the island that the years of data collected from the various implemented projects become a kind of second nature or intuition. In the age of rapid technological advances and computer modeling systems, this ability to have an intimate relationship with the land as conservation workers allows them to use the adaptive management approach effectively. But it also sometimes means becoming emotionally attached to the outcomes.

Sometimes when faced with new changes that present novel challenges, the question of how to adapt is not obvious. In the case of the Laysan ducks, which had only existed on Kuaihelani and Kamole, we were faced with the challenge of stabilizing the introduced population. It didn't stop us from trying.

The ducks on Kuaihelani as well as the ducks established on Hōlanikū have suffered from outbreaks of botulism.

Botulism is a highly toxic illness that affects the nervous system. It is actually considered one of the most lethal substances known in the discipline of epidemiology according to the World Health Organization and can inflict any number of animals, but has widely been documented in avian cases, including translocation efforts such as the Laysan duck.[36]

The toxin is created by spores produced by the bacterium *Clostridium botulinum*. The bacteria itself is common throughout the environment, being resistant to heat, but in oxygen-free environments, such as a deceased animal, they germinate, grow, and excrete the deadly toxin. There are several types of botulism toxins known, and three are known to cause illness in mammals, birds, and fish. The symptoms are quite sad to witness: fatigue, weakness, and vertigo.[37] The ducks are severely impaired when inflicted. If caught in time, a duck with advanced systems can potentially be revived with an administration of antitoxins and fluids. If not discovered in time, a duck can die in as little as twenty-four hours. If a duck dies from botulism, it can become a source of the toxin for other ducks who can eat the maggots that grow in and feed on the decaying carcass.

Before our season in the late winter/early spring, before the ducks began to pair up and mate and hens began settling into their nests, the outgoing winter crew discovered multiple cases of suspected botulism right at the time when they were to be preparing for departure, which was a multiweek process. The plan to finish up their last cycle of habitat treatment to prepare our oncoming crew for a smooth transition was negated. The inflicted adults were brought into

---

36   "Botulism," World Health Organization, last modified January 10, 2018.

37   Ibid.

captivity with the hopes of being able to monitor them closely for developing signs, diagnose the ailment, and treat. Our team anxiously waited for the updates that came through the satellite communication system while we sailed up the chain of islands on the M/V Kahana vessel, hoping for anything good. Instead, we received daily reports, which darkened our hopes. We began to prepare ourselves upon arrival to Hōlanikū for a winter crew that would be a little more tired than usual at the end of their season, and also a little behind on the habitat treatment cycle.

Since those early cases of botulism poisoning in March, the ducks seemed to be doing fine and were actively moving around, busily bouncing between water sources spread across the island—perfectly normal behavior for ducks engaged in the buzz of mating season. It was still a little chilly on those early season days, but during the warming months of late spring and early summer, the busy mating activity of the ducks faded away and the hens disappeared into unknown and hidden nest sites around the island, incubating their eggs for the next twenty-eight days or so.[38]

With the changing seasons, more cases of seabirds were dying, leaving carcass remains behind. We had variable spring weather, fluctuating between hot days that caused a wave of die-offs, with cool rain which collected in puddles on some of the harder substrates of the island. These weather patterns and the effects on the conditions of the island left us feeling anxious, as we knew this was a potential cause for the botulism bacteria to bloom at higher rates, increasing the risk of inflicting the vulnerable Laysan duck population.

---

38 Anna P. Marshall, "Activity Budgets of Captive Laysan Ducklings (Anas Laysanensis)," *Zoo Biology*, no. 11: 353-362 (1992).

The higher temperatures, standing water, and protein source of the carcasses all help to increase the spore production of the bacterium in which the toxin is found.

A day of treatment in the northwest corner of the island came to an end, and on our way back into camp, we split up to do our seep check of the day. Now that the broods had hatched and the ducklings were on the foraging prowl with the hens, it was time for us to monitor the water sources. We had caught a break so far. No signs of botulism present in any of the ducks yet, but we did begin to find dead ducklings at each of the monitoring locations. Ducklings have a naturally low survival rate, often dying from starvation or being separated from their brood. It could not be determined whether botulism was the cause of death, and so there was no reason to suspect the botulism had returned. Only once we discovered signs of botulism in one of the adult ducks did we begin to keep an extra eye out for dead ducks and ducklings, since their carcasses could house the toxin and be spread to the rest of the island's Laysan duck population.

It was only a few weeks before I had discovered the first brood of the season. A hen and her six ducklings were swimming in the Booby Acres guzzler over in the northwest quadrant of the island. I went to check the guzzler, a crafted pond that catches rainwater and stores it in an open container dug into the ground for the ducks to swim about in and drink from. I was looking for mosquitos, a new introduction to the island most likely blown over from Kuaihelani. As I crouched to peer under the roof of the guzzler, which only stood a few feet tall, I witnessed a group of energetic ducklings splashing and playing in the shaded haven. The sudden event of our first brood of the season brought forth a new wave of energy into camp. We had all been keeping our eyes peeled for any signs of hens brooding but had seen nothing until today. The ducklings were already mighty in size, thirteen to eighteen days old by the looks of their prominent necks and developed tail feathers.

Finding the first brood was exhilarating, and to see them at such a developed stage was cause for celebration, for it meant they had surpassed the age of highest risk of mortality. That day we got to celebrate life. Even as we get to live and exist in this wildlife refuge all to ourselves, the nature of our work means witnessing a lot of the inhabitants facing death. It weighed on me. But today our spirits flew high and soared with the *manu* flying in the strong Pacific winds.

Not long after the first brood was logged, we began to find dead ducklings. Worried about the fate of the Laysan duck population on Hōlanikū, we increased our seep and guzzler checks to twice a day. More and more ducklings were being found, collected, and stored in one of the freezers to be brought back to the labs for further examination. I was finding a lot of ducklings, and I wasn't always emotionally prepared for it.

Sometimes I'd be walking to and from an out-planting site and see a fragile little body off to the side. Other times I'd be resting over the weekend, preparing to read a good book and hoping to escape for a little while from the sad news of the ducklings.

Just as I was settling in to read my book, I heard the chirping call of a hen outside my bunkhouse window. It was that special chirp we'd all become familiar with after the broods first started showing up in camp, the hens calling out their vocal signaling as an attempt to keep the ducklings from straying too far. It was the same chirping sound Old Matt and I heard on that Saturday morning when the ducks first began showing up in camp with their broods. I noticed it was R5, identified by a red band around her foot with a "5" etched into it. I went out to see how many ducklings she had. Just yesterday there were five, but today only two. I grabbed my binoculars and radio and started walking around camp to search for the missing ducklings.

I found one almost immediately. It was out in the open sun, lying on its side, panting, drawing in some of its last breaths. I crouched to observe the duckling. It reflexively kicked its legs as my head passed over the sun, casting a shadow over it, contorting its body

The duckling's eyes were half-closed. My heart was pounding.

It was the first time I had found a duckling before it had actually died, but as I watched it contorting its body in a final attempt to move from its fatal position under the sun, I knew there was nothing I could do to save its life.

This little life form, so new to the world, so fragile, was dying right in front of me, and the best I could do was merely acknowledge its existence. In its growing stillness, I imagined it was returning to its egg, to that comforting world from which it came, from where we all come, that place we all share in common.

I sat down against the wall of the bunkhouse, my knees up against my chest.

I waited.

I did not feel saddened by the duckling as it lay dying on the earth of Hōlanikū. I felt content, like it was exactly what I was supposed to be doing. I didn't know how long this duckling had been out in the exposed sun. I didn't know what its mother was feeling as it continued to chirp away in the vicinity, looking for her missing duckling.

I didn't have any answers to explain what to do in that moment as its struggle was coming to an end.

The duckling rolled its head back and then dropped it one last time, and that was it.

The passing of life, the will to live extinguished. I watched it all unfold, the life unraveling into nothingness.

We spend our entire lives facing one adversity after the next, overcoming one struggle after another, fighting to live, fighting to survive, yet all the while knowing in the end, there is no escape from death.

How beautiful. Even as intelligent of a species as our own, imbued with the awareness of our own mortality, of the mortality of all life, we still persevere through it all as if to preserve the element of mystery itself, to cherish existence as something worth, eventually, giving up.

I picked up the duckling, thinking it was dead, and as I carried it back to the freezer to preserve for lab analysis, I felt warmth still clinging to the body, and then a heartbeat. The tiniest, nearly unnoticeable bump against the palm of my hand. Then nothing.

"Goodbyes aren't a single moment," I caught myself saying, trailing off as I continued my walk to the main house.

A TROPIC BIRD'S GUIDE
ON GIVING UP CONTROL

Three weeks remained, three more weeks to leave our mark. The end of a season offers a special kind of excitement for the environmental conservation warrior. Each day forward is one day less to get acreage treated within the cycle. Areas of the island were now taking two to three times longer than they had during the beginning of the season. Our ambition was challenged as we craned our necks and gazed down at all the invasive grasses left to treat.

In the profession of conservation management, control becomes a precarious relationship teetering between the practice of minimal impact on the wildlife while attempting to change only the specific factors identified as the major problem. It is a tricky accommodation. Merely intervening in such environments could bring about unintended consequences for the very wildlife those efforts are trying to restore and protect. But the benefits far outweigh the costs. The presence of habitat restoration technicians on Hōlanikū is undoubtedly saving this island.

Control is embedded within the very technical language we use to describe our work: *control* of invasive species. We use the term to best illustrate our treatment strategy with certain incipient plants observed to cause a reduction in overall biodiversity. Knowing when something needs to be controlled versus eradicated goes a long way in adapting a management strategy sustainable for both the island and the habitat technicians who are implementing the work.

Nature constantly incorporates new variables and the species making up any given system constantly struggle to maintain their existence; each mode of life pursues its own genetic success. Yet when we zoom out, we see every species plays a special role in maintaining the existence of the entire natural system.

For example, every spring the bumblebee, *Bombus terrestris,* fulfills its niche in nature pollinating plants. It's an example of how the selfish gene, as Dawkins puts it, somehow adds up to a collective equilibrium.[39] The genes of this bumblebee enable it to work ferociously every day in collecting the syrupy offerings of nearby plants, which, in turn, allows the bee to flourish and for the plants it pollinates along the

---

39   Richard Dawkins, *The Selfish Gene* (United Kingdom: University of Oxford Press, 1976).

way to succeed in reproduction. Neither the bee nor the plant has come to a mutual agreement to help each other out. In fact, these species have evolved tactics to take advantage of the presence of each other in their shared environment to succeed over other species who may share a similar niche. This equilibrium is not static; it is constantly changing, and when a new species is introduced to a new world, the equilibrium can be compromised.

We came here to restore the island, a now year-round presence of specially trained workers doing their best to reduce their impact while attempting to reshape the vegetation for all of the island's inhabitants. Every day our team of six people (now that Young Matt joined us mid-season) trekked across the island in search of the invasive plants, fully knowing we would be met with an onslaught of newly sprouted mats of plants. In the short term, it could be discouraging.

After returning to a site we had treated multiple times throughout the season, it looked like we had not made a dent. But the truth was the nature of this work is about persistence, looking ahead, understanding growth cycles, and continuing forward at whatever pace sustains our long-term efforts. The data recorded over the many years of restoration efforts indicates many of the invasive plants found on the island are on the decline or have already been eradicated. It is also a little more complex than invasive or nonnatives being bad, and noninvasive or natives being good.

There are some detrimental native Hawaiian plants like *kauna'oa pehu, Cassytha filiformis,* a vine whose parasitic nature began to compromise the vital dune structures of parts of the island by growing on the essential *naupaka* and killing it. There are advantageous nonnative plants like some of the grasses growing on the island who have proven to be beneficial to recovering the habitat of certain areas by preventing more invasive plants, like the *verbesina,* from growing.

Overall, Hōlanikū is a success story, one which can be used to help other management programs learn how to identify the specific needs of their own natural areas.

One of the elements contributing to the conservation success of this atoll is the effort of the team. Our team was composed of a group of deeply committed workers spanning the full spectrum of experience, from veteran managers who had been coming out to Hōlanikū for a decade to new volunteers who had never been to Hawaiʻi.

I fell somewhere in the middle. My prior experience on the atoll gave me a vantage point, but I still could not quite see the bigger picture. The visibility of our efforts came in cycles. Sometimes we were getting somewhere. Other times we were going in circles. We couldn't accomplish everything in a single season. Already the atoll had changed so much due to the numerous camps that worked the winter and summer seasons before us. Those continuous efforts had already placed Hōlanikū into the relatively stable state it is today. We were just the next vital step in continuing this process. No matter how much it seemed like not much had changed over the last five months, we were part of a bigger trend toward success.

But some days didn't feel like that. Some days we had to let that vision of success go to give in to the present struggles chasing us down.

***

On a particularly hot day in a particularly challenging restoration area of the island, my focus started to fade. My skin and the plastic watch face on my wrist were stained with a combination of sun exposure, salty sweat, and debris—2:00 p.m. I tried calculating how long it had been since we started, but my mind wasn't cooperating. I was thirsty and out of snacks.

Running out of water, or snacks, may seem like a small thing, especially given there was plenty of water and snacks to be found back at camp or in our resupply wheelbarrow, but it is still taken seriously by the team leaders. The team leaders incorporate practices such as mandatory water breaks at predetermined intervals as well as asking us to announce the team leaders when we have depleted our provisions. There is also a ritual checking of snacks and water before everyone sets out into the field for the day.

I squeezed my eyes shut, gathering the fortitude for basic arithmetic. *Five hours.* We'd been treating a steady mat of invasive plants hiding under the thick *naupaka* for five hours straight.

These invasive species found in Hōlanikū are common enough in most of the world, even intentionally used for projects such as landscape design installations. Plants like sweet alyssum, *Lobularia maritima*, which blooms lovely tiny white flowers with a sweet scent as its name suggests, attract pollinators to aesthetic yards and outdoor displays. I had once used *L. maritima* while working in a native plant nursery to help attract pollinators.

But on the island, *L. maritima* takes on a very different growth characteristic, rapidly colonizing open areas in such a way that natives struggle to compete. Its drought-tolerant taproot system and prolific seed production express its advantage thoroughly and effectively. The plant itself does not appear to be directly harmful to wildlife, which is how it would have looked to those who first brought it to Hōlanikū—more of a harmless decoration. Fast-forward forty years and the plant has established itself all over the island. Wiping out a plant all at once is not feasible, so instead, the strategy is to control the population, allowing an opportunity for the plants we are trying to promote to establish themselves.

The last time we had treated this specific restoration area (RA), Sector Five West, it had taken only three hours. I whipped out my GPS and the digital map of the RA. My track line mapped the route I took: a squiggly zigzag bouncing between my neighbors on my left and on my right, ending at the point where I now stood, less than halfway through the entire RA.

I looked for the newest member of our team, Young Matt. He was staring off into the distance like he was trying to sniff out a breeze in the stagnant heat of the *naupaka* bush, which was so thick it blocked any wind that might have been blowing in from the ocean. He was pale and a thin line of sweat formed where his recently shaved mustache once stood. He was looking tired. Today we crossed into new territory; this was the longest we had ever gone in a single RA, and its end was nowhere in sight.

I slipped the GPS back into its harness, exchanging it with my radio, holding it like a lever to a dynamite ignition box. I hesitated. I felt my shallow breath expire from my lungs. The radio felt heavy. I rubbed the sweat collecting on my forehead and then pushed the talk button. I let the waves reach the other radios, searching for diplomatic words while battling a low throb marching across my head.

Young Matt snagged his foot in a branch, sending him crashing forward. A forgiving *naupaka* broke his fall but also entangled him and triggered a group of nesting red-footed boobies into a croaking frenzy.

I shouted over the *'a* into the radio. "Jon-Erik to Old Matt, Jon-Erik to Old Matt, I'm just looking at our progress here and it looks like we still have got quite a bit left. I'm also looking at the clock and wondering what you think about breaking for lunch."

A big part of our job as trained habitat restoration technicians working in an extremely remote environment is to know when to make the call, when to change the original plan. But even as experienced professionals, finding the right answer to a given situation isn't always obvious. Sometimes when something feels so close to grasping, it is better to just push through. But sometimes the right call is to stop and pick it up another time. Sometimes that decision is not immediately apparent, nor mutually apparent among the group.

"Yeah, copy that." There was brief radio silence in what I gathered was a tone of dismay, or maybe it was a familiar sound of fatigue that accompanied us during the end of a season. His voice came back over the radio. Our whole team could hear him. "I think we should call it if everyone can find a good stopping point. Better to stop now so we have a good chunk to come back to and finish tomorrow."

Young Matt, who had managed to untangle and upright himself, met up with me. We clambered out of Sector Five West toward the open and more forgiving air on the runway, an old airstrip leftover from the Coast Guard days. Now it acted as a corridor for us to access the island's south side. It also proved to be an effective runway for the albatross who required a bit of a running start to take off into flight. Young Matt expressed his uncertainty with the decision. Tired as he looked, he was determined to charge ahead so we did not have to go back a second time.

He had a point. The thought of going back in didn't sit right. It was the only area left to treat on the far side of the runway, one of the furthest areas from camp. Granted, it was a small island that only stretched a couple of miles across but wheeling all of our supplies down the entire length of the old airway strip was not the most efficient way to spend our time. It took about twenty minutes to walk from camp, forty minutes round trip, and we were already feeling anxious about losing precious daylight hours.

Young Matt and I discussed our retreat as we trampled over the slippery limbs of the *naupaka*. I was starting to feel unsure about my decision to get on the radio and throw a wrench in our day's objectives. But the deed was done. The word was out. The call was made.

One by one, we awkwardly made our way out of the *naupaka* thicket stretching between the beach and the runway. I could tell I was not the only one feeling unsure about our derailment.

We started to shuffle back toward camp in silence, heads drooped slightly lower. The wind from the east hit our drenched clothes, providing some relief from the heat we had just endured. The heels of my boots scraped against the rough substrate of the runway. It extended ahead of us for what looked like miles. But we all knew the exact distance: four thousand feet. We had walked it countless times throughout the season and marked every thousand feet with buoys collected from the beach. Now it seemed those deep pockets of *naupaka* were closing in from both sides of the endless, bleach-white runway, separating us from those plastic buoys sizzling in the heat waves on the island's scorched surface.

We passed albatross chicks in their thick, downy feathers, panting, all facing eerily in the same direction, beaks pointed away from the glaring sun with their webbed feet lifted as much as possible off the searing ground.

Far ahead of the group Naomi, the other camp leader, stopped and faced us. I couldn't tell what emotion she was wearing behind the dark, reflective sunglasses she always wore. Naomi, who normally carried a song in her step, stood in the way of our path back to camp.

"I'm pretty dissatisfied," she finally exclaimed. No one answered, and I realized I was supposed to say something as the one who got on the radio.

"What are you dissatisfied with?"

I knew the answer when we were still back in the *naupaka*. Being our team leader, as the veteran of the group and the one with the most blood, sweat, and tears invested in the revival of this droplet of land in the middle of the Pacific Ocean, Naomi felt this island more than any of us. Her emotions broke into her voice.

"I didn't get closure in there. I think we should just finish it."

The screech of a red-tailed tropicbird, *koaʻeʻula*, rocketed over my head. The binding spell of Naomi's words broke, alerted to the chase of four determined great frigate birds, *iwa*, pursuing their frantic victim. The *koaʻeʻula* screamed, cutting sharply right and angling away from the stealers, but one of the *iwa's* predicted this move, and, with a more powerful and dynamic wingspan, it snatched at the tropicbird, latching onto its feathers with her hooked beak.

The *koaʻeʻula* twisted its neck and lashed back at the *iwa*, able to break free, but the *iwa* were fast on her trail.

Naomi spoke out again. "What do you all think if we go back for lunch, then come back out here in the afternoon?"

I gazed back down from the chase in the sky to respond, trying to sound level-headed. "If we are going to go back to camp, I don't think we'll have much time to come all the way back out here today."

A poignant screech echoed from above, and we all looked up to see the *iwa* had caught the *koaʻeʻula*, again, but this time its hooked beak held on, fastened to the *koaʻeʻula's* tail feathers. The *iwa* swooped further up into the sky with its powerful, arched wings, the *koaʻeʻula* flailing wildly about, her screeches bellowing across the atoll. Alas, the *koaʻeʻula* was overwhelmed, throwing up its food that only seconds ago was digesting nicely in the acids of her stomach. A fish fell from the sky, shimmering silver as it caught the light of the sun. The group of *iwa* hovering nearby, poised for this very moment, dove down toward the cascading fish carcass.

Our back-and-forth continued, fueled by the expected fatigue that settled on our crew of worked bodies, provoking untempered emotions. Everyone had something to say, all with a tone of tired impatience. Time was wasting away as we stood in a circle surrounding an invisible point of tension, which kept us anchored in place, struggling to accept what was already occurring in the middle of the runway.

The motivation to not give up had lost its appeal. It was a motivation I had used to feel secure. The hope to succeed had been chased into exasperation. Now it had been caught, and there was no escaping except to give up the control that came with holding on to an outcome, and let it fall unto the fate of the island's humbling powers.

The fastest out of the *iwa* outmaneuvered the rest and snatched the half-digested fish out of midair just before it hit the ground. It was an aerobatic feat with a finale worth applause. The *koaʻeʻula*, although freed of the panicked harassment, was now empty of sustenance and flew away to safety and hunger, unnoticed by the *iwa*.

There is no one thing in control. Everything is happening together. The coevolution of the *iwa* and *koaʻeʻula* is a good example of this. The *iwa*, with its larger and more aerial-adapted wings, evolved to chase other birds down and force them to give up their food, and the *koaʻeʻula* evolved to give up its food. It isn't ideal, and from our human perspective down here on the ground it may seem unfair, but the *iwa* don't see it that way, and perhaps neither do the *koaʻeʻula*. Sometimes the *koaʻeʻula* will fly away, better off giving up control of its food than to continue exhausting its energy fighting off the *iwa*.

We never went back into Sector 5 West. It would have to wait until tomorrow. With the conclusion of the *iwa* and *koaʻeʻula* event, we unbuckled our spray packs, placing them in the wheelbarrows, and walked back to camp where a late but much-needed lunch would await us under the cool concrete fixture of the old main house. Refueled, rejuvenated, and resolved of the hard decision to call it quits, things didn't seem so tough anymore. We had failed today's objective, but we were better for it.

And so was Hōlanikū.

CONCLUSION—THE GREAT JOURNEY BEYOND

It was August: hurricane season. School had just started. A large storm was heading our way. I had only just begun teaching, maybe a week or two, when the storm hit Hawaiʻi Island. It was uncertain what the storm would do when it arrived, so the schools proactively closed. I spent five days alone in my cabin. It was the first time I had with myself, unable to go anywhere, unable to do anything but confront my brother's death.

* * *

Time felt eternal on Hōlanikū. But its eternity was only a spell broken by the early morning crackling of the radio and the voice of the captain of the M/V Kahana announcing their arrival back to the atoll. They were here to drop off the incoming winter team and to pick up our outgoing summer team.

I returned to the main Hawaiian Islands in the fall of 2017, ready to begin a path back toward guiding adolescence into adulthood. But rather than find a rites-of-passage program, I looked toward the education system. Less than a year later, I found myself standing in front of a class of tenth graders, back in Hilo Hawaiʻi, teaching English Language Arts.

One of the last things I remember my brother telling me was how much he hated school but loved to learn. I think perhaps those words more than any other gave me the courage and purpose to become a teacher. Maybe I could make a difference for all those students who were like my brother.

It was only a month after he died. I had been back home with my family in Seattle. We were all huddled together in the house we all grew up in—that my parents raised us in—just taking care of each other, just being taken care of. I didn't know quite what life was going to be like returning to Hawaiʻi. I felt, more than anything, afraid.

I got the call from the high school asking if I wanted to interview for a position that opened up for the new school year. After the interview, they called the next day and offered me the job. I accepted the position as a full-time teacher, finally fulfilling a goal I had made upon returning from Hōlanikū.

Less than a week later, I was standing in front of my class of tenth graders, dressed in a button-up shirt with neatly groomed hair.

* * *

When the storm hit, it slowed to a near standstill, hovering over sections of the island. Rain came cascading down all around me. The skies were perpetually darkened. I could not leave my neighborhood, for the roads out to the highway were flooded. I could no longer ignore the present thoughts of the absence of my brother.

I began to imagine my brother after death. I began to envision the journey that comes beyond the world of the living.

I imagined him as a ghost—his existence now only logged memories in my mind, past murmurs reverberating in my heart. He was no longer beside me but, instead, a subtle force behind me. I could still sense him and maybe, just maybe, if I turned around quickly enough, I might catch a glimmer of his image.

I imagined him next wandering across the vast landscapes of this Earth in loneliness, surrounded by life but no longer a part of it, only moving through it but moving past it, fading out of existence and into nothingness. The closer he tried to move toward something he knew, the more he would come to find his own tangibility would dissolve. He has accepted his severance from the living, but not from home. He still attempts to walk among the planes of this world from which he existed as Taiga. So he wanders, not yet ready to answer the call to a greater cosmic universe awaiting him. Perhaps this was what my brother was doing now, visiting the places he never got to, holding on as tight as he can to the only world he knew, yet slowly losing his grasp—slipping away.

* * *

A student's response to a prompt I gave my class just days before came flashing through my mind. She shared a metaphor for how her mind works.

"It's the tides," she said, "ebbing and flowing."

It made me think of my brother standing along the edge of the shore, the intertidal zone, which makes up one of the harshest ecosystems on the planet because of the constant nature of change—the desiccation, salinity, and wave turbulence. It is very much a world between worlds—not quite land, not quite the sea.

I imagined my brother making it to the shore after wandering aimlessly as a lost spirit on Earth. I imagined him splitting from the memories he has attached all of his existence to and severed from. I imagined his own notion of himself shrinking and dissolving into the rocky shore, becoming detritus for the invertebrates to consume, breakdown, and assimilate back into the Earth.

I imagined the pain of all this and the grief he must have felt to no longer have a life. We the living mourn what we have lost, but what of the dead? How do the dead mourn?

The sun, bringer and destroyer of life, Brahma, rises between the dividing and splitting of his existence, severing my brother once and for all from any more ties to this earthly plane. It is time to never look back.

* * *

I gazed out at my class ten weeks later after my first day. My students had returned from fall break. I had gone home to visit my family. It just so happened the week-long break coincided with my parents' birthday (my mother and father have the same birthday)—and my brother's. It was our first birthday without him. He would have turned twenty-one. That visit home changed everything.

They were finishing another journal writing prompt. Today's was: *write about a time in your life when you didn't know what the right thing to do was.*

"I have something to share with you all," I started to say as the last few pens scratched across their journals. Hardly anyone looked up. They had no idea what was to come. How could they? I never told them about my brother. I didn't want it to get in the way of my professional work. I was afraid if I did then I would no longer be able to be a source of strength for them, but rather my vulnerabilities would show I was in no position to be taking on a new role as a teacher.

"I'd like to share a time in my life when I didn't know what to do. Actually, this time is now." A number of heads now looked up. Some looked intrigued, others concerned. "In June, my younger brother died. I was home all summer but came back to start this position as your teacher. I thought I could move past the shock and pain of it all, but I haven't. I need time. I didn't know what to do. I couldn't abandon you all, but I don't feel like I can continue on living away from my family like this. I want to apologize to you all. I have decided it is time for me to move back home. I don't know what is going to happen, or if I'll ever return. I also don't know if this is the right choice. But you have already changed my life, and I hope one day I will at the very least return to teaching."

They were upset, but they understood. They asked about my brother. How old was he? How did he die? I had never experienced so much compassion in my life. Nearly every student came up to me, from every class, sharing a moment with words of care.

"It's okay, mister. You gotta do what you gotta do."

"We understand. Go be with your family."

"We'll miss you mister, but we'll be okay."

"You're a good teacher; you better become a teacher back in Seattle!"

Two years later, and I have not yet returned to teaching. But their voices still ring in my head, cheering me on.

* * *

The sound of the rain has drowned out all other thoughts but those of my brother. My memories of him began pouring down. The trip my brother took to visit me in Hawai'i surfaced. My brother peering into Mauna Ulu grabbed a hold of me. I sat in the small room of my cabin and awaited the moment I would sense my brother discovering his liberation into the vast unknown, the uncharted territories we mere mortals have only seen through the eyes of our instruments.

I imagined him discovering all that exists beyond, like when he looked down into the crater of Mauna Ulu. My brother leaning ever so slightly down toward the depth of creation, while still holding onto the earthen rock, made me think of that moment we discover just how deep the rabbit hole goes.

When we confront the aspects of ourselves that no longer serve us, and only after shedding the dead, dry skin, are we ready to face the chapters in life beckoning us forth. Perhaps the end of life is only the shedding of our physical burden to be released into a greater chapter of existence. The excitement building like the twitching of a cat's tail before lunging into action is a sense that triggers the awakening of every molecule in our being. For the dead, what exists that can feel, if anything?

I imagined him taking the great leap, *paulele*, into the great universe, now a traveler of the cosmos. I imagined the joy as he was at last on his way toward the infinite, rocketing through the heavens, exhilarated by this newfound freedom.

I imagined him navigating fields of celestial bodies. He would become a cosmic cartographer, mapping the endless skies, becoming in death all he could not in life, preparing a world we would someday all find our way to. The great journey beyond.

I will only miss you here on this earth for a brief moment, for life is short. In this brief moment that remains of my life, I have eternity to look forward to spending with you.

GLOSSARY

Aʻali ʻi - native Hawaiian hopseed bush; *Dodonaea viscosa*

Aliʻi - chief, chiefess

Āhinahina - silver sword endemic to Hawaiʻi; *Argyroxiphium kauense*

Akulikuli - sea purslane; *Sesuvium portulacastrum*

Ao - Light, day, daylight, dawn; to dawn; grow light, enlightened; to regain consciousness

ʻApapane - Hawaiian honey creeper; *Himatione sanguinea*

Hala - pandanus; *Pandanus tectorius.*

Halau - used to establish a hula group, among other types of groups, or a physical housing for a specific use

Haleakala - volcano of Maui Island

Hamakua - district on the North side of Hawaiʻi Island

Haumea - Hawaiian Goddess of fertility, Pele's mother

Hawaiʻiloa - ocean channel between Nihoa and Mokumanamana

Halemaʻumaʻu - crater within Kilaeua volcano; home to Pele

Haole - used to describe a foreigner, or more precisely a white person

Hilo - city on Hawaiʻi Island

Hōlanikū - Kure Atoll

Honolulu - city on Oʻahu Island

Honu - green sea turtle

Honuaʻieakea - the mythic canoe Pele travels upon to Hawaiʻi

Hula - ritual dance

Huliau - overturning or complete change.

Ike - knowledge

Iwa - great frigatebird; *Fregata minor*

Iwi - bone, carcass

Kahana - turning point, Rebirth

Kahiki - Tahiti, place of origin

Kaho'olawe - island of Hawai'i

Kai - ocean

Kamani - *Calophyllum inophyllum*

Kanaka - human being

Kānehoalani - god who rules the heavens

Kauna'oa pehu - native parasitic vine to Hawai'i; *Cassytha filiformis*

Ka'upu - black-footed albatross; *Phoebastria nigripes*

Kawelu - grass native to Hawai'i; *Eragrostis variabilis*

Keaukaha - coastal region in the Hilo district of Hawai'i Island

Kilauea - volcano on Hawai'i Island

Koa – native tree endemic to Hawai'i

Koa'e kea - white-tailed tropicbird; *Phaethon lepturus*

Koa'e'ula - red-tailed tropic bird; *Phaethon rubricauda*

Ko'olau - mountain range on O'ahu Island

Kuaihelani - Midway Atoll

Kuahu - altar

Kumukahi - eastern-most point of Hawai'i Island

Kumulipō - a selection of Hawaiian creation chants

Lāhui - nation, race, tribe, people, nationality

Laka - Hawaiian goddess of the forest

Lāna'i - island of Hawai'i

Lani - sky, heaven

Lehua - flower

Lei - garland, wreath usually made of plants. Traditionally, made of plants from the native forests of Hawai'i for use in hula, as well as other material collected from nature

Loulu - endemic palm to Hawai'i; *Pritchardia hillebrandii*

Mana - supernatural or divine power

Manu - bird

Manu o kū - white-tern; *Gygis alba*

Maui - island of Hawai'i

Mauna - mountain

Mauna Kea - volcano of Hawai'i Island

Mauna Loa - volcano of Hawai'i Island

Mauna Ulu - volcano, part of the Kilauea volcano of Hawai'i Island

Mokumanamana - Necker Island of the Northwestern Hawaiian Island

Moku O Keawe - Hawai'i Island

Moloka'i - island of Hawai'i

Mō'ī - king, sovereign, monarch

Mōlī - Laysan albatross; *Phoebastria immutabilis*

Mo'okū'auhau – genealogy

Mo'olelo - story

Nāmakaoakaha'i - Pele's older sister

Naupaka - coastal shrub native to Hawai'i; *Scaevola taccada*

Nihoa - Nihoa, Island of the Northwestern Hawaiian Island

Noio kōhā - brown noddy; *Anous stolidus*

O'ahu - island of Hawai'i

'Ōhi'a - endemic tree to Hawai'i; *Metrosideros polymorpha*

Palapalai - native fern to Hawai'i; *Microlepia strigosa*

Palikapuokamohoali'i - the name of a cliff that overlooks Kilauea caldera

Paulele - a leap of faith, trusting fully in something

Pele - Hawaiian goddess of fire

Pō - night, darkness, obscurity

Pōʻele - one half of the first binary pair in the Kumulipō that represent a class of plants and animals coming into creation

Pōheʻenalumamao - one half of the binary pair in the second half of the Kumulipō in which the manifestation of is ao

Pōkinikini - one half of the binary pair in the second half of the Kumulipō in which the manifestation of is ao

Pōpolo - black nightshade; *Solanum nigrum*

Pukiawe - native Hawaiian Heather; *Leptecophylla tameiameiae*

Puna - region in Hawaiʻi Island where much of the Kilauea volcano resides

Puna Luʻu - black sand beach on Hawaiʻi Island in the district of Kaʻu

Puʻu Oʻo - a very active crater that is part of Kilauea volcano on Hawaiʻi Island

ʻUaʻu kani - wedge-tailed shearwater; *Puffinus pacificus*

Uhu - parrot fish; Family: *Scaridae*

Waʻa - canoe

Wai - water

Waikiki - district in the Honolulu

Wailele - waterfall

Waimanu - valley in Hawaiʻi Island

Waipiʻo- valley in Hawaiʻi Island

Wana - multiple species of sea urchin; *Diadema paucispinum, Echinothrix diadema, Echinothrix calamaris*

ACKNOWLEDGMENTS

———

I don't know if I would have written this book if there were not countless people in my life encouraging me to do so. The amount of support I had before starting this endeavor allowed me to believe that, yes, this was something I could do. Once I began, in came a whole other set of people who helped shape this into its completed form. Without them, I never would have finished. I have learned so much along the way while writing *Return to Pō*, more than I bargained for. I now have a sense of what it means to create something and put it out into the world. Thank you to all who made it possible.

Thank you first and foremost to my family and friends for supporting me every step of the way. For taking me on long runs in the mountains where I could process all I was writing. For reminding me why I decided to write this in the first place every time I wanted to put it down and walk away. For challenging me to go the extra mile and making sure it was as it should be. For holding me accountable.

Thank you to the Creators Institute and New Degree Press for approaching me about writing a book. You brought what was living as a fantasy in my mind into the real world. Thank you to Eric Koester for believing everyone has a story worth publishing. Thank you to my editors Robert K. and Elina O., and the rest of New Degree Press.

Thank you, Matt and Naomi, for your editing contributions, for being my friends, my mentors, and for your dedication to Kure Atoll. Thank you, Cynthia, for helping to edit all of the biological content. I am incredibly grateful for your willingness to help.

Thank you, Nimz, for creating the internal graphics as well as the *Return to Pō* sticker. You are the biggest support a fellow Kurean could ask for.

Thank you, Mom, for editing and supporting me in more ways than one.

Thank you, Dad, for editing and inspiring me to follow in your footsteps.

Thank you, Grandpa, for your generous support throughout.

Thank you, Katherine, Eleanor, and Josephine, for believing in me.

Thank you, Taapai, for every moment we have shared.

Thank you, Papa, for always helping me see things more clearly.

Thank you, Shelby, for keeping me going during the hardest moments.

Thank you, Stan, for inspiring me to write and to find my love for writing.

Thank you to everyone who shares these memories with me.

Lastly, thank you to everyone who pre-ordered the eBook, paperback, and multiple copies to make publishing possible, helped spread the word about *Return to Pō* to gather amazing momentum, and help me publish a book I am proud of. I am sincerely grateful for all of your help:

Adam Arafat
A'i DiMarco
Alec Richardson
Alex Dorros
Alexa Davis
Alexander Marts
Allison Vincler
Amanda Juvinall
Amy Dong
Anna Pollema
Anna Sparks

Benjamin Aron Mayer
Benjamin C Gregory
Benjamin J Kramer
Benjamin Schmechel
Billy Barnett
Brian Coon
Bodhitaraishere
Bonnie Moses
Brant Hinckley
Bree Brown

Carter Lawrence
Carver Low
Cary Stidham
Chase Watson
Chaunda Malia Rodrigues
Cheryl Riess
Chuck Tookey
Chyanne Garcia
Colin Hume

David Ashe
David Voeller
Deanna Amodeo
Denise Ventre

Edward Ury
Eric Koester
Erin Jones
Erin Libsack
Evan Pearson

Fran Hartung Nunes

Gatnats
Granny Lambert

Hana Stern
Hayley Umayam
Holly Eberhart

Izaac Holt

James A Hinckley
James M Hughes
James Morioka
Jen Hartke
Jenise Rouse
Jesse Corrington
Jesse Potter
Jessica Eskelsen
Jessica Torvik

Lauri Leach

Joe Barcia
John Heinekey
Josephine Jardine
Jourdan Hinkle
Julia Shure
Julie Parish
Jung Amaral
Justin Manson

Kara Flowers
Karen Hinckley Stukovsky
Karen Wood
Karin Grafstrom
Katelyn Steen
Katherine Jardine
Katherine Mayor
Katie Voeller
K. Golden
Kimberly Gerhardt
Kris Brown
Kyle E Norris

Lachlan Huck
Laura Dvorak
Lauren Tran
Leah Kerschner
Leo Shallat
Lisa Gibert
Liza Higbee-Robinson
Lynn Beasley

Madeline Kennedy
Massimo Marchiano
Matt Fogel
Max Schellhorn
M. C. Foley
Michael Pretsch
Michelle Quast
Michelle Smith
Mimi Peradotto
Miriam Schwartz
Monica Hinckley

Nathan Weinstein
Neil Rasp
Nick Adair

Ilana Nimz

David Golden

Noah Lee-Engel

Olivia Hill

Patrick & Sara Stover
Patrick Vizard
Phillip Farris

Ray Bailis
Rebecca J Jordan
Regina Fletcher
Rena Behar

Robb Grimes
Robert E Irr
Robyn Trivette
Ryan Della

Sarah E. Johnson
Sarah Youngren
Shari Frias
Shelby Woods
Shirley Urman
Smokey Zilch
Sue Schuler
Stan Tag

Mary Sullivan

Tara Kaena
Tobias Kuhn
Toby Harris
Tyler Sprague

Virginie A. Ternisien

Will Ryan

Zina Hottovy

APPENDIX

AUTHOR'S NOTE

Kikiloi, Kekuewa Scott T. "Kūkulu Manamana: Ritual Power and Religious Expansion in Hawai'i." PhD diss., University of Hawai'i at Manoa, 2012.

WHO I AM IS WHERE I AM

Emerson, Nathaniel Bright. *Pele and Hiiaka: A Myth from Hawaii.* Hilo: Edith Kanaka'ole Foundation, 2015.

Nimmo, Harry. *Pele, Volcano Goddess of Hawai'i: A History.* Jefferson: McFarland & Company, Inc., Publishers, 2011.

WAVES OF WAIMANU

Campbell, Joseph. *The Hero with a Thousand Faces.* Navato, California: New World Library, 2008.

Fire, John, and Richard Erdoes. *Lame Deer: Seeker of Visions.* New York: Simon Schuster, 1994.

Gennep, Arnold van. *The Rites of Passage Second Edition.* Translated by Monika B. Vizedom and Gabriel L. Caffee. Chicago: University of Chicago Press, 2019.

Katz, Richard, Megan Biesele, and Verna St. Denis. *Healing Makes Our Hearts Happy: Spirituality and Cultural Transformation Among the Kalahari Ju|'hoansi.* Rochester: Inner Traditions International, 1997.

Sopolsky, Robert. *Why Zebras Don't Get Ulcers.* New York: Henry Holt and Company, LLC, 1994.

Turner, Victor W. *The Forest of Symbols.* New York: Cornell University Press, 1967.

Wilber, Kenneth. A *Theory of Everything.* Berkeley: Shambhala Publications, 2000.

ALL THE WAY UP THE CHAIN TO HŌLANIKŪ

Prahbupāda, A.C. Bhaktivedanta Swami. *Bhagavad-Gita as It Is.* *The Bhaktivedanta Book Trust International, Inc. August 2012.* Kindle.

THE ISLAND AND THE CANOE

Hoʻomanawanui, Kuʻualoha. *Voices of Fire: Reweaving the Literary Lei of Pele and Hiʻiaka.* Minneapolis: University of Minnesota Press, 2014.

Kikiloi, Kekuewa Scott T. "Kūkulu Manamana: Ritual Power and Religious Expansion in Hawaiʻi." PhD diss., University of Hawaiʻi at Manoa, 2012.

National Academy of Sciences. "Evolution in Hawaii: A Supplement to 'Teaching About Evolution and the Nature of Science.'"

Washington, DC: The National Academies Press, 2004. https://doi.org/10.17226/10865.

National Geographic. "Atoll." Accessed September 16, 2020. https://www.nationalgeographic.org/encyclopedia/atoll/.

Papahanaumokuakea Marine National Monument. "Papahānaumokuākea as a Refuge for Rare and Globally Significant Species." Accessed July 30, 2020. https://www.papahanaumokuakea.gov/wheritage/refuge.html.

DEPARTURES AND ARRIVALS

Duffy, David Cameron. "Changing Seabird Management in Hawaiʻi: from Exploitation through Management to Restoration." *Waterbirds* 33, no. 2 (June 1, 2010). https://doi.org/10.1675/063.033.0208.

Kikiloi, Kekuewa Scott T. "Kūkulu Manamana: Ritual Power and Religious Expansion in Hawaiʻi." PhD diss., University of Hawaiʻi at Manoa, 2012.

DEATH OF OUR LIVES

Fischer, J., and D.B. Lindenmayer. "An Assessment of the Published Results of Animal Relocations." *Biological Conservation* 96, no. 1 (November 2000).

Marshall, Ann P. "Activity Budgets of Captive Laysan Ducklings (Anas Laysanensis)." *Zoo Biology*, no. 11 (1992).

Sutton, Alexandra E., and Roel Lopez. "Findings from a Survey of Wildlife Reintroduction Practitioners." *F1000Research* 3, no. 29 (January 29, 2014).

World Health Organization. "Botulism." Last modified January 10, 2018. https://www.who.int/news-room/fact-sheets/detail/botulism.

A TROPICBIRD'S GUIDE TO GIVING UP CONTROL

Dawkins, Richard. *The Selfish Gene*. United Kingdom: University of Oxford Press, 1976.